CLASSIC *f*M

The *Friendly* Guide to

Film Music

Rob Weinberg

The publisher has used its best endeavours to ensure that the URLs for external websites referred to in this book are correct and active at the time of going to press. However, the publisher has no responsibility for the websites and can give no guarantee that a site will remain live or that the content is or will remain appropriate.

For UK order enquiries: please contact Bookpoint Ltd, 130 Milton Park, Abingdon, Oxon OX14 4SB. Telephone: +44(0) 1235 827720. Fax: +44(0) 1235 400454. Lines are open 09.00–17.00, Monday to Saturday, with a 24-hour message answering service. You can also order through our website www.hoddereducation.com

British Library Cataloguing in Publication Data: a catalogue record for this title is available from the British Library.

First published in UK 2009, by Hodder Education, 338 Euston Road, London NW1 3BH.

Copyright © 2009 Rob Weinberg

Typeset by Servis Filmsetting Ltd, Stockport, Cheshire
Printed in Great Britain for Hodder Education, part of Hachette UK, 338 Euston Road, London NW1 3BH, by CPI Cox & Wyman, Reading, Berkshire RG1 8EX.

Hachette UK's policy is to use papers that are natural, renewable and recyclable products and made from wood grown in sustainable forests. The logging and manufacturing processes are expected to conform to the environmental regulations of the country of origin.

Impression number   10 9 8 7 6 5 4 3 2 1

Year   2013 2012 2011 2010 2009

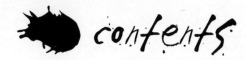

contents

A Friendly Word Before We Get Started

If you've just picked this book up in a shop – or even already bought it – you've probably realized by now that we're on a journey to find out more about film music.

Since our launch in 1992, we at Classic FM have always enjoyed making links between classical music and the movies. The first contact many of us had with the great classics – barring commercials for Hovis – was when Mickey Mouse struggled to tame his wayward broom in *Fantasia*'s "*Sorcerer's*

Apprentice" sequence. Or perhaps your first encounter with Wagner took place while his "*Ride of the Valkyries*" boomed out of Chinook helicopters thundering over Vietnam in *Apocalypse Now*.

Throughout the past century, while so-called "serious" composers often shunned melody, beauty and harmony, film composers were creating some of the most melodic, dramatic and inspirational orchestral music ever written. All of them were equally serious about their craft, many of them classically trained and trying to earn a living while often continuing to write for the concert hall. Many classical composers, starting with Saint-Saëns and coming up to date with Philip Glass, have created music for the big screen.

Classic FM proudly showcases film music every day in its programmes. Specifically, each weekend for more than a decade, *Classic FM at the Movies*, presented by Simon Bates, has featured the greatest soundtracks, exciting new releases and the world's favourite classical pieces as heard in the movies.

So we'll make no apology to the classical purists for giving film music the credit and exposure it deserves. It not only contributes to a great experience at the cinema – enhancing the excitement and inspiring emotions – but it also opens the world of great orchestral and choral music to the biggest imaginable audience.

A natural evolution

The creation of music by great composers has always gone hand in hand with two things – the telling of stories and the demands of the patron. The earliest pieces that survive are the settings of scripture or liturgy for the church and monastery – music deliberately designed to enhance the spiritual and emotional journey for worshippers. At the same time, troubadours were roaming the land or based in court, singing songs of love and loss. By the 16th century, wealthy patrons were demanding all sorts of music for every occasion. Madrigal singers perfected the art of "word painting", matching their music to the meaning of the words.

Opera arrived at the beginning of the Baroque era and, inspired by ancient Greek drama, composers collaborated with writers and directors to tell stories, fusing music with theatrical spectacle. Vast sums of money were spent on costumes, lighting and stage effects. Singers became the superstars of their day. All the while, the nobility demanded more and more music to entertain their guests.

During the "classical era", composers broke away a little from being mere servants to their noble masters or the church. They earned their own money but still responded to commissions from those who held the purse strings. Without such patronage, we would never have had Haydn's *The*

Creation or Mozart's *Don Giovanni*. Like the best films, Mozart's or Rossini's finest operas explore the complexity of human relationships and contain music that supports the action and emotions of the characters.

The "romantic era" saw musicians experimenting with all sorts of new musical ideas. Great composers, such as Beethoven, were often commissioned to provide incidental music for the theatre. Storytelling through descriptive music is perhaps best typified by Berlioz in his *Symphonie fantastique*. Wagner caused a revolution creating a genre of opera that perfectly fused every element of the arts. Puccini understood the power that music has to make audiences weep with sadness or gasp in horror.

It was only to be expected then, with the arrival of film, that music would play a major role in accompanying the telling of stories on screen. Film was the natural evolution of the kind of storytelling for the masses pioneered by the troubadour and the great opera composers, taking in literature and theatre along the way. Filmmakers have been eager to employ the best composers to increase the emotional experience, just as the church did centuries before. And what a back catalogue of classics they also had to draw upon! It seems natural to think that had Beethoven or Mozart been living in our time they would have enthusiastically embraced composing for the cinema and probably now computer games as well. Many up-and-coming film composers have cut their teeth in the world of games.

Film music is still in its earliest years – roughly only a century old. So it's remarkable that so many film themes have rapidly become loved the world over, with a life of their own outside the cinema in the concert hall and on disc. The majority of music lovers – whatever their favourite genre – would not hesitate to call the theme to *Schindler's List* or *Lawrence of Arabia* classics. This *Friendly Guide* celebrates such works and the remarkably talented composers who brought them into existence.

How to use this *Friendly Guide*

This book is designed to give you an overview into film music's development – from cinema's silent era up to the most successful composers of today. It would be impossible to include all the music that has been created for the cinema in the past 100 years but we've tried to concentrate on the key figures who've shaped its evolution and whose work you'll hear most often on *Classic FM at the Movies* and elsewhere on Classic FM.

After the timeline in Chapter 1, which allows you to see where the great film composers fit in alongside significant landmarks in cinema and soundtrack history, the next six chapters take you

on a chronological journey. You will find a handy "At a glance" guide to most of the main composers in the grey boxes throughout these chapters.

Chapter 8 explores the relationship between classical music and the cinema, including works created by great classical composers for the cinema, as well as listing some of the pieces that have been put to use – and in some cases found a new lease of life – in films. There's also a look at classical music stars on celluloid.

The next chapter, entitled "That's All, Folks!" turns the spotlight on some of the geniuses who've written music for animated films over the decades, as well as exploring cartoonists' ongoing love affair with classical music.

Chapter 10 is a selection of quotes from film composers, talking about their craft and each other. This is followed by a chapter entitled "100 Masters of Movie Music", providing an A–Z listing of 100 key composers in the history of cinema and their major works. The scores that have won Academy Awards® – both in the USA and UK – are listed in Chapter 12. Film music that has appeared in the Classic FM Hall of the Fame, the annual poll of our listeners' 300 favourite works, can be found in Chapter 13.

This book comes with a CD of especially selected music, which you will find on the inside cover. The

CD contains 20 essential movie tracks – 10 written especially for the cinema and 10 popular classics that have been used in films. Chapter 14 tells you more about these timeless pieces.

At the back of the book, we've tried to provide a comprehensive list of further reading – websites, magazines and journals – should you be a full-blown film music fanatic by the time you get there. There's also a glossary of musical terms, as well as the names of artists, filmmakers and composers that pop up in the text, as well as an index of all the composers mentioned.

We wanted to make our guide as friendly on the eye as possible, so we have adopted the same style that we have used in the other books in this series:

- titles of all films and musical works are set in italics
- songs and arias appear in italics within quotation marks.

We hope that your knowledge and enjoyment of film music is greatly enhanced by this *Friendly Guide*. And we hope that you'll come to share our view that film music is to be counted among the greatest music ever written.

The Friendly Guide to Who Was Composing When

This timeline brings together in one place all of the composers featured in our *Friendly Guide to Film Music*, allowing you to see how film music was created against the backdrop of developments in cinema history.

YEAR	Who was born?	Who died?	Cinema and soundtrack landmarks
1887	Oliver Wallace		
1888	Max Steiner Roy Webb		The very first moving picture sequence (of traffic in Leeds) is shown in public
1889	Charles Chaplin		
1890			
1891	Arthur Bliss Sergei Prokofiev Carl Stalling		The Edison company demonstrates the Kinetoscope, a single viewer peepshow device
1892	Arthur Honegger		
1893			
1894	Dimitri Tiomkin		
1895			The Lumière brothers patent the *Cinématographe* camera and projector and put on the first public paying performance
1896	Hans J. Salter		Edison launches Vitascope, the USA's first commercially successful projector
1897	Adolph Deutsch Erich Wolfgang Korngold		
1898			
1899	Georges Auric Victor Young		

YEAR	Who was born?	Who died?	Cinema and soundtrack landmarks
1900	George Antheil Aaron Copland		
1901	Daniele Amfitheatrof Frank Churchill Hugo Friedhofer Alfred Newman		
1902	Bronislau Kaper William Walton		The first permanent movie house designed for showing motion pictures built in Los Angeles Georges Méliès produces *Le Voyage dans la Lune*, the first science-fiction film
1903	Aram Khachaturian		First western film, *The Great Train Robbery* Charles Pathé becomes dominant figure in French film industry
1904	Richard Addinsell		
1905	William Alwyn Alan Rawsthorne		
1906	Benjamin Frankel Anton Karas Dmitry Shostakovich Franz Waxman		Earliest surviving example of animated film made – the 3-minute *Humorous Phases of Funny Faces* World's first feature-length film, *The Story of the Kelly Gang*, premieres in Australia
1907	Leigh Harline Miklós Rózsa		First European feature-length film, *L'Enfant Prodigue*

CONTINUED ▶

3

YEAR	Who was born?	Who died?	Cinema and soundtrack landmarks
1908			Saint-Saëns composes the first totally original film score for *L'Assassinat du Duc de Guise*
1909	Brian Easdale		*New York Times* coins the term "stars" for leading movie players
1910	Alex North		First film companies move into Hollywood
1911	Bernard Herrmann Nino Rota		
1912	David Raksin		Mack Sennet begins production of first Keystone comedies *Queen Elizabeth*, starring Sarah Bernhardt, released in USA
1913	Jerome Moross Mario Nascimbene		
1914			Charles Chaplin's first film, *Making a Living*, released First feature-length colour film, *The World, the Flesh and the Devil*, premieres in London
1915			D.W. Griffith's 3-hour civil war epic, *Birth of a Nation*, premieres
1916			*Intolerance* Samuel Goldfish (later Goldwyn) and Edgar Selwyn establish Goldwyn Company
1917	Robert Farnon		John Ford makes first film, *The Tornado*
1918	Leonard Bernstein		The Warner Brothers – Jack, Albert, Harry and Samuel – open their first studio First *Tarzan* film premieres

YEAR	Who was born?	Who died?	Cinema and soundtrack landmarks
1919			Charles Chaplin, D.W. Griffith, Douglas Fairbanks and Mary Pickford establish United Artists
			The Cabinet of Dr Caligari; *Broken Blossoms*
			First appearance of Felix the Cat
1920	John Addison		Douglas Fairbanks stars in *The Mark of Zorro*
	Ravi Shankar		
1921	Malcolm Arnold	Camille Saint-Saëns	
1922	Elmer Bernstein		*Nanook of the North* is first feature film documentary
			F.W. Murnau's *Nosferatu*
1923			Cecil B. DeMille's *The Ten Commandments* is the most expensive film ever made
1924	Maurice Jarre		Walt Disney directs first short, *Alice's Wonderland*
	Henry Mancini		Erich von Stroheim's *Greed*
	Leonard Rosenman		MGM studios formed from three US film production companies
1925	James Bernard		Sergei Eisenstein's *Battleship Potemkin*
	Georges Delerue		*Ben-Hur* released, costing $3.95 million and grossing $9 million on first release
	Ron Goodwin		Chaplin's *The Gold Rush*
	Robert B. Sherman		*The Phantom of the Opera* with Lon Chaney Sr
	Mikis Theodorakis		*The Lost World* uses stop-motion special effects of dinosaurs
1926		Rudolph Valentino	*Don Juan* is first publicly shown "talkie" with synchronized sound effects and music

CONTINUED ▶

5

YEAR	Who was born?	Who died?	Cinema and soundtrack landmarks
1927			*The Jazz Singer* is the first widely screened feature-length talkie The first sound news film, Fox's *Movietone* newsreel, shows Lindbergh's trans-Atlantic flight Fritz Lang's *Metropolis*; Buster Keaton's *The General* Abel Gance's *Napoleon* experiments with wide-screen and multi-screen effects
1928	Ennio Morricone Richard M. Sherman		First Mickey Mouse film, *Plane Crazy*, debuts. The sound *Steamboat Willie* is released later Paramount becomes first studio to produce only "talkies" King Vidor's *The Crowd*; *Un chien andalou* by Luis Buñuel and Salvador Dali
1929	Jerry Goldsmith		First Academy Awards® announced First original musical released, *The Broadway Melody* The Marx Brothers' first film, *The Cocoanuts*, premieres Hitchcock's first sound film, *Blackmail*, is released
1930	Toru Takemitsu		*Little Caesar* is first talkie gangster film Garbo talks, in *Anna Christie*, *All Quiet on the Western Front* Howard Hawks' *Scarface*
1931	Malcolm Williamson		*Dracula*, with Bela Lugosi, and *Frankenstein*, with Boris Karloff, premiere Fritz Lang's *M*; Charlie Chaplin's *City Lights*

YEAR	Who was born?	Who died?	Cinema and soundtrack landmarks
1932	Wojciech Kilar Francis Lai Michel Legrand Lalo Schifrin John Williams		Disney's Technicolor *Flowers and Trees* is the first in the *Silly Symphonies* series Shirley Temple's career begins Jean Renoir's *Boudu sauvé des eaux*
1933	Luis Bacalov John Barry Stanley Myers		Fred Astaire and Ginger Rogers dance in their first joint movie together, *Flying Down to Rio* *King Kong* includes groundbreaking feature-length musical score by Max Steiner *42nd Street* saves Warners from bankruptcy
1934			*It Happened One Night* sweeps the Academy Awards®, winning the five major awards Donald Duck debuts in *The Wise Little Hen*
1935			Century Pictures and Fox Films merge to form 20th Century Fox Max Steiner's score for *The Informer* becomes major influence on other soundtracks *The Bride of Frankenstein*
1936	Richard Rodney Bennett Carl Davis		Composer Carl Stalling chooses "The Merry-Go-Round broke down" as Warners' cartoon theme George Cukor's *Camille*; *Things to Come* has Arthur Bliss score
1937	Angelo Badalamenti Philip Glass Jack Nitzsche	George Gershwin	Disney releases *Snow White and the Seven Dwarfs*, the first feature-length animated film

CONTINUED ▶

7

YEAR	Who was born?	Who died?	Cinema and soundtrack landmarks
1938	Howard Blake John Corigliano		*Alexander Nevsky* premieres with score by Prokofiev *The Adventures of Robin Hood*
1939			"The greatest year in film history" – *Gone with the Wind, Ninotchka, Mr Smith Goes to Washington, Stagecoach, The Wizard of Oz* and *Wuthering Heights* all released
1940	Richard Robbins		Disney releases *Pinocchio*, the first film with an "original soundtrack" album *Fantasia* introduces a multi-channel soundtrack and successfully mixes animation with classical music John Ford's *The Grapes of Wrath*; *The Philadelphia Story* Bugs Bunny says "What's up Doc?" for the first time; Tom and Jerry debut
1941	Pino Donaggio		*Citizen Kane* launches Orson Welles' and Bernard Herrmann's film careers Greta Garbo retires at 36 *The Maltese Falcon* is the first detective film to use the *film noir* style
1942	Bill Conti	Frank Churchill	*Casablanca* premieres in New York Orson Welles directs *The Magnificent Ambersons*
1943	Randy Newman Jean-Claude Petit Vangelis		Luchino Visconti's *Ossessione*

YEAR	Who was born?	Who died?	Cinema and soundtrack landmarks
1944	Karl Jenkins Michael Nyman		*Double Indemnity* is the peak of *film noir* *Henry V* with William Walton's score
1945	Basil Poledouris Philippe Sarde		Rossellini's *Rome, Open City* introduces Italian neo-realism Marcel Carné's *Les enfants du paradis* Hollywood's first musical biopic, *Night and Day*, stars Cary Grant as Cole Porter *Spellbound*; *Mildred Pierce*
1946	Howard Shore		Billy Wilder's *The Lost Weekend* wins the top prize at the Cannes Film Festival Cocteau *La belle et la bête*; *Black Narcissus*; *Great Expectations* *Brief Encounter* uses Rachmaninov's 2nd Piano Concerto
1947	Randy Edelman		*The Best Years of Our Lives* wins Oscars® for Best Picture, Best Director and Best Supporting Actor
1948	John Carpenter Michael Kamen Ilona Sekacz		Olivier's *Hamlet* with music by Walton becomes the first non-American film to win Best Picture Oscar® *Letter from an Unknown Woman*; *The Red Shoes*
1949	Alan Menken Gabriel Yared		*The Heiress* with score by Aaron Copland; *Kind Hearts and Coronets* *The Third Man* with music by Anton Karas; Leonard Bernstein's *On the Town*
1950	George Fenton Peter Gabriel Alan Silvestri		Kurosawa's *Rashomon* Billy Wilder's *Sunset Boulevard* *All About Eve* is released – it later picks up a record 14 Academy Award® nominations

CONTINUED ▶

YEAR	Who was born?	Who died?	Cinema and soundtrack landmarks
1951	James Newton Howard Gustavo Santaolalla		*The Thing* and *The Day the Earth Stood Still* launch craze for sci-fi films *A Streetcar named Desire*, *The African Queen*
1952	Ryuichi Sakamoto		*Singin' in the Rain*
1953	Patrick Doyle Danny Elfman James Horner Jan A.P. Kaczmarek Stephen Warbeck	Arnold Bax Sergei Prokofiev	Oscars® televized for the first time Ida Lupino directs *The Hitch-Hiker* *Shane* released – later nominated for five Oscars® *From Here to Eternity*
1954	Elliot Goldenthal David Newman Barrington Pheloung Trevor Rabin		Fellini's *La Strada*; *Rear Window* *Animal Farm* is the first colour animated feature film made in England Dorothy Dandridge nominated for Best Actress Oscar® for *Carmen Jones* *On the Waterfront* wins eight Oscars® Kurosawa's *The Seven Samurai*
1955	Carter Burwell Ludovico Einaudi Thomas Newman	Arthur Honegger James Dean	*Blackboard Jungle* is first film to feature a rock'n'roll song *The Cobweb* has Hollywood's first atonal film score, by Leonard Rosenman
1956	Patrick Cassidy Anne Dudley	Victor Young	*Forbidden Planet* and *Invasion of the Body Snatchers* released Cecil B. DeMille remakes *The Ten Commandments* *The Searchers*

YEAR	Who was born?	Who died?	Cinema and soundtrack landmarks
1957	Tan Dun Don Davis Hans Zimmer	Erich Wolfgang Korngold	Bergman's *The Seventh Seal* is released *The Bridge on the River Kwai* with score by Malcolm Arnold
1958	Howard Goodall Zbigniew Preisner	Alan Rawsthorne Ralph Vaughan-Williams	Hitchcock's *Vertigo* *The Big Country*; Hammer's *Dracula*
1959	Craig Armstrong Eric Serra Marc Shaiman	George Antheil	The French "new wave" gets underway with Chabrol's *Le beau Serge* *Ben-Hur* released, before winning 11 Oscars® *North by Northwest*; *Some Like it Hot*
1960	David Hirschfelder Jocelyn Pook Rachel Portman		Hitchcock's *Psycho* Kubrick's *Spartacus* Fellini's *La Dolce Vita*
1961	Alexandre Desplat Lisa Gerrard Harry Gregson-Williams		*West Side Story* adapted for the big screen *Jules et Jim*
1962	David Arnold Terence Blanchard	Marilyn Monroe	*Dr No* marks James Bond's first appearance Kubrick's *Lolita*; *How the West was Won*; *To Kill a Mockingbird*; *Lawrence of Arabia*
1963	Dario Marianelli John Powell Debbie Wiseman	Oliver Wallace	Sidney Poitier becomes first black actor to win Best Actor Oscar®, for *Lilies of the Field* *Cleopatra*, the most expensive film ever made, opens . . . and flops *It's a Mad Mad Mad Mad World*; *The Great Escape*, *The Pink Panther*

CONTINUED ▶

YEAR	Who was born?	Who died?	Cinema and soundtrack landmarks
1964	John Ottman		*A Hard Day's Night; Goldfinger; My Fair Lady; Dr Strangelove*
1965			*The Sound of Music* premieres and becomes the number one box office hit of all time *Dr Zhivago* with Maurice Jarre score
1966	A.R. Rahman		*Who's Afraid of Virginia Woolf?*: is the first film containing extreme language and sexual content Antonioni's *Blow Up; The Good, the Bad and the Ugly*
1967	Michael Giacchino	Franz Waxman	*A Fistful of Dollars; Belle de jour; The Graduate*
1968	Klaus Badelt		*2001: A Space Odyssey* reinvents the science-fiction genre *Planet of the Apes*
1969		Leigh Harline	*Midnight Cowboy; Easy Rider; The Wild Bunch; Kes*
1970	Yann Tiersen	Alfred Newman	Disaster movies begin with *Airport* *Love Story; M*A*S*H*
1971		Alan Rawsthorne Max Steiner	*A Clockwork Orange, Walkabout, Straw Dogs*
1972		Carl Stalling	*The Godfather* released *Last Tango in Paris; Deliverance*
1973		Benjamin Frankel	*The Exorcist; Mean Streets; Don't Look Now* Bob Dylan writes the score for *Pat Garrett and Billy the Kid*
1974			Polanski's *Chinatown; The Godfather Part II*

YEAR	Who was born?	Who died?	Cinema and soundtrack landmarks
1975		Arthur Bliss Bernard Herrmann Dmitry Shostakovich	*One Flew Over the Cuckoo's Nest* wins all the major Oscars® *Jaws; Barry Lyndon*
1976			*Taxi Driver; The Omen; Rocky*
1977		Richard Addinsell Charles Chaplin	*Star Wars; Close Encounters of the Third Kind; Annie Hall;* *Saturday Night Fever*
1978		Aram Khachaturian	*Grease; The Deer Hunter; Hallowe'en*
1979		Adolph Deutsch Nino Rota	*Apocalypse Now; Alien; Manhattan; Kramer vs Kramer; Mad Max*
1980		Dimitri Tiomkin Alfred Hitchcock	*Raging Bull; The Shining; The Elephant Man*
1981		Hugo Friedhofer	*Chariots of Fire; Raiders of the Lost Ark*
1982		Roy Webb	*Star Trek II: The Wrath of Khan* is first film to use computer- generated images Disney's *Tron* contains more than 20 minutes of computer animation *ET: The Extra-Terrestrial; Blade Runner; Fitzcarraldo; Gandhi*
1983		Georges Auric Bronislau Kaper Jerome Moross William Walton	*The Right Stuff; Fanny and Alexander; Koyaanisqatsi* with Philip Glass score; *Once Upon a Time in America*
1984			*Amadeus; Ghost Busters; A Passage to India*

CONTINUED ▶

13

YEAR	Who was born?	Who died?	Cinema and soundtrack landmarks
1985		William Alwyn Anton Karas	Back to the Future; Out of Africa; Ran; Brazil; The Colour Purple
1986			Pixar Animation Studios becomes an independent company A Room with a View; Platoon; The Mission; The Fly
1987			The Untouchables; Moonstruck
1988			Die Hard; The Last Temptation of Christ; Cinema Paradiso
1989			Tim Burton's Batman is the box office smash of the year Classic Disney animation is revived with The Little Mermaid Glory; My Left Foot
1990		Leonard Bernstein Aaron Copland	Pretty Woman; Dances with Wolves; Edward Scissorhands
1991		Alex North	Disney's Beauty and the Beast is the first animated film to be nominated for Best Picture Oscar® The Silence of the Lambs
1992		Georges Delerue	Aladdin; Reservoir Dogs
1993		Stanley Myers	Schindler's List; The Piano; Groundhog Day; Jurassic Park; Short Cuts
1994		Henry Mancini Hans J. Salter	The Lion King; The Shawshank Redemption; Four Weddings and a Funeral; Pulp Fiction Forrest Gump uses digital photo technology to insert Tom Hanks into historical footage
1995		Brian Easdale Miklós Rózsa	Toy Story is the first totally digital feature-length animated film Braveheart; Se7en; The Usual Suspects

YEAR	Who was born?	Who died?	Cinema and soundtrack landmarks
1996		Toru Takemitsu	*Fargo; Shine; The English Patient*
1997			*Titanic*, the most expensive film of all time, becomes the highest grossing film in Hollywood history
1998		John Addison	*Saving Private Ryan; Life is Beautiful; Shakespeare in Love*
1999			*The Matrix; Magnolia; The Sixth Sense; American Beauty; Fight Club*
2000		Jack Nitzsche	*Crouching Tiger, Hidden Dragon; Chicken Run; Gladiator; Memento*
2001		James Bernard	*Shrek; A Beautiful Mind; Amelie; Spirited Away; Moulin Rouge*
2002		Mario Nascimbene	*The Pianist; Gangs of New York; Hero*
2003		Ron Goodwin / Michael Kamen / Malcolm Williamson	*The Return of the King; Finding Nemo*
2004		Elmer Bernstein / Jerry Goldsmith / David Raksin	*The Incredibles; The Passion of the Christ; Million Dollar Baby*
2005		Robert Farnon	*Brokeback Mountain; Cinderella Man; Munich*
2006		Malcolm Arnold / Basil Poledouris	*Casino Royale; The Queen*
2007			*Babel; Atonement*
2008		Leonard Rosenman	*The Dark Knight; WALL*E; Slumdog Millionaire*
2009		Maurice Jarre	

02

Pioneering Days

It might seem ironic to begin the story of film
music with silent movies. But, in fact, cinema's love
affair with music – and classical music in particular
– dates way back to the era before the "talkies"
arrived. Today, silent movie buffs even argue that
theirs was the golden age, when the music was
foreground, not background, music, played live in
the movie theatre. In those days, it didn't have to
fight to be heard over sound effects and dialogue.

It's hard to pinpoint an exact date when music
began to be heard in picture houses. As early as the
1890s, some short films may even have had a pianist
sitting in front of the screen playing along to the
moving pictures. Certainly, in December 1895, the

Lumière family tested out some of its films in Paris with a piano accompaniment. By April 1896, several London venues were showing films accompanied by a full orchestra. But it's also claimed by some that the music was there for a very practical purpose – to drown out the noise made by the projector!

In those early days, little thought was given to fitting the music to the drama up on the screen, as pianists banged their way through a selection of irrelevant ragtime tunes. It was also handy to have a pianist around tickling the ivories to keep the audience happy while the film was being rewound or new spools were loaded up.

As audiences became more sophisticated, so, too, did the demands on the music that went with the cinemagoing experience. Generally, it was left up to the musicians to choose whatever music they wanted or plunder the classical repertoire – or both. Very often, whole extracts were lifted from the works of Beethoven or Tchaikovsky. But even as early as 1904, the light operetta composer and conductor **Herman Finck** (1872–1939) was employed as a music director in London writing accompanying music to films, as well as editing selections of classical favourites to be performed by orchestras in cinemas.

Film companies later began sending out "cue sheets" with the reels, listing the major scenes of the film, their approximate length and suggestions for appropriate pieces of music. Each cinema's musical director could hunt out the appropriate pieces, put them in order or, if he didn't have the exact piece, stick in something similar in mood. Consequently, cinemas built up huge music libraries comprising thousands of works.

It was only a few years before classical composers were approached to create scores for movies. **Camille Saint-Saëns** (1835–1921) was probably the first famous name to provide a score to a film. In 1908, he wrote the music for the 18-minute long production, *L'Assassinat du Duc de Guise*. Its producers, who had also encouraged well-known stage actors to perform in their films to give them some kudos, made a big deal about promoting the fact that Saint-Saëns had provided music for their movie. He later developed his music for *L'Assassinat* into a concert work – the Opus 128 for strings, piano and harmonium.

In 1910, Pathé sent out a complete piano score to accompany its film of *Il Trovatore*. The music was even sold commercially but was not a huge success. By 1914, the Oz Film Manufacturing Company's films had original scores written by **Louis F. Gottschalk**.

Gottschalk was a friend of the writer L. Frank Baum, creator of *The Wizard of Oz*. Together

> ## At a glance: Louis Gottschalk
>
> Born: 1864
> Died: 1934
> Must listen: *The Four Horseman of the Apocalypse* (1921),
>   *The Three Musketeers* (1921), *Orphans of the*
>   *Storm* (1921)

they formed the Oz Film Manufacturing Company. Gottschalk wrote four complete scores for Baum at a time when cinema musicians mostly used cue sheets. The composer progressed to working with D.W. Griffith, arranging cue sheets for *Broken Blossoms* (1919) and scoring *Orphans of the Storm*.

A former pupil of Dvořák's, **John Stepan Zamecnik** (1872–1953), published the seminal "Sam Fox Moving Picture Music, Volume 1" in 1913. The first widely published sheet music for silent film accompaniment, the volume consisted of 23 pieces for piano, covering the most needed backing pieces for comedies and melodramas. The book and its sequels remained bestsellers throughout the entire silent film era. By 1920, as films became feature length, Zamecnik created pieces to suit longer, more dramatically complex scenes. He eventually moved to Hollywood where, uncredited, he created full-length original scores for such films as *Wings* (1927), *The Wedding March* (1928), *Redskin* (1929) and *Betrayal* (1929).

Two other composers of cue music for the silents worth remembering were:

- Frenchman **Irénée Bergé** (1867–1926). Bergé studied with Massenet before becoming a chorus master at Covent Garden in London and a prolific composer of cantatas and orchestral music. His music designed to accompany silent movies included albums of oriental suites and various dance pieces.
- **Gaston Borch** (1871–1926). Borch was an accomplished cellist and conductor who also studied with Massenet. His music for cinema orchestras in a wide range of styles included aptly titled pieces such as "Dramatic Tensions" and "Pathetic Andantes".

Most of the composers of the silent era are now forgotten. They received no credit for their compositions, their music was never recorded and then, to cap it all, the medium they worked in died with the coming of sound. Some, though, are ripe for rediscovery.

At a glance: Hugo Riesenfeld

Born:	1879
Died:	1939
Must listen:	*Carmen* (1915), *Beau Geste* (1926), *The King of Kings* (1927), *Make a Wish* (1937)

Vienna-born **Hugo Riesenfeld** moved to the USA with opera impresario Oscar Hammerstein I and worked with his Manhattan Opera Company. Riesenfeld worked on the score for Raoul Walsh's silent version of *Carmen* (1915) and served as musical director for United Artists Pictures from 1917–1925 before moving on to Fox, Paramount and other studios. He composed music for more than 60 movies and had a particular gift for incorporating classical music and popular songs into his scores.

Ernö Rapée (1891–1945) was assistant conductor to Riesenfeld at the Rialto Theatre in New York. During that time he began conducting for silent films on Broadway. In 1923, Rapée's compositions were published under the banner of the "Capitol Photoplay Series". His pieces *"Frozen North"*, *"The Clown's Carnival"* and *"Pollywog's Frolic"* are popular examples of the music written to accompany silent movies. Rapée and Riesenfeld published their manuscript sources in *Rapée's Encyclopedia of Moods and Motives for Motion Pictures*.

Edmund Meisel (1894–1930) wrote scores for Sergei Eisenstein's *Battleship Potemkin* (1925) and *Ten Days that Shook the World* (1928). His score for *Potemkin* was not the first or, indeed, only music written for the film. However, standing out from his contemporaries, Meisel's version demonstrated a profound understanding of the power that music has to enhance the action on the screen.

D.W. Griffith's controversial film *The Birth of a Nation* (1915) broke new ground in film scoring. It was one of the first attempts to create a score specifically for a single picture. Griffith's main collaborator was **Joseph Carl Briel** (1870–1926), who combined folk melodies and well-known classical selections – including Wagner's *"Ride of the Valkyries"* – into some 214 separate music cues. At its premiere, *The Birth of a Nation* was screened with an orchestra of almost 100 musicians and 12 singers.

Charles Chaplin was the first global superstar, thanks to the movies. He directed, scripted, produced and wrote music for his own films.

At a glance: Charles Chaplin

Born:	1889
Died:	1977
Must listen:	*The Gold Rush* (1925), *The Circus* (1928), *City Lights* (1931), *Modern Times* (1936)

Claude Debussy sought out Charles Chaplin in Paris and told him he was "instinctively a musician and a dancer". Among the other composers that Chaplin counted as friends were Rachmaninov, Stravinsky and Schoenberg. But Chaplin had no musical training and couldn't read or write music. He often sang his tunes for others to write down.

As early as *A Woman of Paris* (1923), Chaplin was taking a close interest in the music for his films. Despite the arrival of sound, he continued to make

silent films. *City Lights* and *Modern Times* are essentially silents, but with the addition of music and sound effects. Chaplin said:

One happy thing about sound was that I could control the music, so I composed my own.

A modern master of silent film music

Before leaving the subject of silent cinema, we should mention one composer whose contribution to providing soundtracks to silent movies is second to none, **Carl Davis**.

At a glance: Carl Davis

Born: 1936

Must listen: *Broken Blossoms* (1919/1983 re-release), *City Lights* (1931/1989 re-release), *Greed* (1924/1986 re-release), *Ben-Hur* (1925/1987 re-release), *Napoleon* (1927/1980 re-release), *The Crowd* (1928/1981 re-release)

Since 1980, when Channel 4 television began a series of restored prints of classic silent films, Carl Davis has provided magnificent scores to more than 50 of them. In 1983, after a Paris screening of Abel Gance's epic *Napoleon,* Davis was honoured with the order of Chevalier des Arts et des Lettres. Live cinema performances of silent classics with Davis scores continue to take place regularly around the world.

Technology changes the movies

Experiments had been going on matching film to recorded music since motion pictures began. In England, in 1900, a short film of a music hall star called *Little Tich and his Big Boots* was released and screened with a recorded orchestral score on disc. Various systems competed with each other before the First World War, which stalled developments. In 1923, the Phonofilm system introduced the idea of recording a soundtrack on a narrow strip down one side of the film. The Fox studios purchased the patent and, combining it with other patents from Germany, created the Movietone system. Warner Brothers and Western Electric developed Vitaphone with impressive results.

By August 1926, Warner Brothers had put together a sound disc of synchronized music played by the New York Philharmonic Orchestra – as well as basic sound effects – to play alongside the premiere of *Don Juan* starring John Barrymore. The next year, the major studios agreed to hold back on their sound experiments until they could decide on one effective system. In June 1927, a Fox newsreel showing Charles Lindbergh's solo non-stop flight from New York to Paris included sound and caused great excitement. In October of that year, *The Jazz*

Singer, starring Al Jolson, changed everything. The public went mad for the film's four Vitaphone segments and Warner's moved completely to sound film production.

With the arrival of sound pictures, classical music became a regular fixture in movies. The first European feature film with a synchronized vocal performance, *I Kiss Your Hand, Madame* (1929), featured the celebrated Austrian tenor Richard Tauber providing the voice to the leading man.

While the movies had made use of music since their very first days, it took an Austrian-born émigré by the name of Max Steiner to take film music to its next stage – what's been called the Golden Age of Hollywood film scores.

The Golden Age

The Golden Age of Hollywood film music – all swashbuckling adventures, *film noir* thrillers, and sweeping romantic dramas – actually began with a giant ape. *King Kong* (1933) launched a new era in which film scores became an even more important part of the cinemagoing experience. *Kong* also helped establish the reputation of the "father of film music", **Max Steiner**, one of the most brilliant of all movie composers. He was nominated for Academy Awards® more than 20 times and won three.

Born in Vienna, Max Steiner was a child prodigy who studied with Brahms and Mahler and had Richard Strauss for a godfather. By the time he was 20, he was earning a living as a conductor and

At a glance: Max Steiner

Born: 1888

Died: 1971

Must listen: *King Kong* (1933), *The Informer* (1935), *She* (1935), *The Charge of the Light Brigade* (1936), *Gone with the Wind* (1939), *The Letter* (1940), *The Great Lie* (1941), *Casablanca* (1942), *Now Voyager* (1942), *The Adventures of Mark Twain* (1944), *Since You Went Away* (1944), *The Flame and the Arrow* (1951), *The Caine Mutiny* (1954), *Battle Cry* (1955)

theatre composer. He left Austria for Britain and then the USA, working as an orchestrator and conductor on Broadway for 11 years.

Steiner arrived in Hollywood just as the major studios were embracing sound. Producer David O. Selznick commissioned him to write the first fully integrated film score – for *Symphony of Six Million* (1932) – revolutionizing the movie industry's approach to music. For *King Kong*, Steiner's grand symphonic score, particularly the use of a three-note theme depicting the beast, set the standard for everything that was to follow.

Steiner took his compositions seriously, making extensive use of the *leitmotif* – a technique favoured by Wagner in which musical phrases are linked to particular characters and used even when they are not on screen to subliminally suggest their presence. *King Kong* also introduced the idea of giving a film an overture and exit music, previewing or, at the end, reprising the score's main themes. For *Casablanca*, Steiner's use of an older Broadway show tune, *"As Time Goes By"*, gave the film a unique atmosphere.

Another onetime child prodigy from central Europe who set the standard for film scoring was **Erich Wolfgang Korngold**. The composer of only 16 soundtracks, it is for his music for Errol Flynn adventures that Korngold is best remembered.

At a glance: Erich Wolfgang Korngold

Born: 1897

Died: 1957

Must listen: *Captain Blood* (1935), *Anthony Adverse* (1936), *The Adventures of Robin Hood* (1938), *The Private Lives of Elizabeth and Essex* (1939), *The Sea Hawk* (1940), *Kings Row* (1941)

Korngold wrote his first orchestral music as a teenager and, like Steiner, also won adulation from the likes of Richard Strauss. Mahler described the young Korngold as a "musical genius". He wrote chamber music, a piano concerto and four operas, including the haunting *Die tote Stadt* that played at the Metropolitan Opera House in New York in 1921. In 1934, Korngold was invited to Hollywood to arrange Mendelssohn's music for a star-studded production of *A Midsummer Night's Dream*. The following year, the composer signed a contract with Warner Brothers. *Captain Blood* launched both his and Errol Flynn's careers properly. Korngold continued to mix film work with concert pieces until Hitler annexed Austria. Then, Korngold moved his family to the USA and concentrated exclusively on film scores, vowing not to write concert works again until Hitler fell.

Korngold combined huge skill and intelligence in his film music. It's bold, brassy, exciting and, at times, heart-wrenchingly romantic. Based on his experience working in the theatre in Vienna, he had an instinctive sense of what worked dramatically and musically. He often took the liberty of telling a producer where a scene should go or even asked for more footage to extend a scene to fit his music.

After the Second World War, with swashbucklers out of fashion, Korngold returned to Europe to resume his concert music career but found himself forgotten in his homeland.

Movie music legend **Alfred Newman** was not only a great film composer – he wielded more power than any of his contemporaries.

At a glance: Alfred Newman

Born:	1900
Died:	1970
Must listen:	*Arrowsmith* (1931), *The Bowery* (1933), *Dead End* (1937), *The Prisoner of Zenda* (1937), *Alexander's Ragtime Band* (1938), *Gunga Din* (1939), *Wuthering Heights* (1939), *The Grapes of Wrath* (1940), *Tin Pan Alley* (1940), *The Song of Bernadette* (1943), *Captain from Castile* (1947), *How the West was Won* (1962), *The Greatest Story Ever Told* (1965)

As a child, Newman played the vaudeville circuit as "The Marvelous Boy Pianist". In his 20s, he worked on Broadway, conducting stage musicals by Gershwin, Richard Rodgers and Jerome Kern. In 1930, Newman travelled to Hollywood with Irving Berlin and had private lessons with Arnold Schoenberg.

Newman was head of music at 20th Century Fox for two decades. There, he pioneered a method of synchronizing the film with the recording and performance of its score, known as the "Newman System", which is still in use today. Newman scored more than 250 films, won nine Oscars® and created a dynasty of Hollywood film composers – his brothers Emil and Lionel were also in the business. His sons David and Thomas are both successful contemporary movie composers, as is his nephew Randy.

Newman's greatest scores were for portentous religious epics, replete with heavenly choirs and shimmering strings. His score for *The Song of Bernadette* became one of the first actual film scores to be released on record, rather than re-recorded for commercial release. Newman was also the composer responsible for the famous 20th Century Fox fanfare – now best known as the prelude to the *Star Wars* theme tune.

Over at Paramount Studios, **Victor Young** was another classically trained composer. Young understood the power of releasing records of soundtracks to boost a movie's popularity and the studio coffers.

At a glance: Victor Young

Born: 1899
Died: 1956
Must listen: *Golden Boy* (1939), *For Whom the Bell Tolls* (1943), *The Uninvited* (1944), *Love Letters* (1945), *Samson and Delilah* (1949), *The Greatest Show on Earth* (1952), *The Quiet Man* (1952), *Shane* (1952), *Around the World in Eighty Days* (1956)

Young was equally successful as a composer of popular songs and light music and his song "*Stella by Starlight*" from *The Uninvited* was recorded numerous times by artists such as Ella Fitzgerald, Frank Sinatra and Ray Charles. Young holds the record for the most nominations received before winning an Oscar® – on his 22nd attempt, for *Around the World in Eighty Days*. Unfortunately, he died before the awards ceremony.

In great demand as an orchestrator and composer, **Hugo Friedhofer** started life accompanying silent films and stage shows. He was brought to the attention of Korngold and was hired by Warner Brothers to arrange and orchestrate scores for both Steiner and Korngold.

At a glance: Hugo Friedhofer

Born: 1901
Died: 1981
Must listen: *The Best Years of our Lives* (1946), *Joan of Arc* (1948), *An Affair to Remember* (1957), *The Young Lions* (1958)

Friedhofer's first full composing credit was for *The Adventures of Marco Polo* (1938). He worked uncredited on more than 120 films. When he finally broke free of anonymity and arranging other people's music, he hit the jackpot with *The Best Years of Our Lives*, a touching score that won him an Oscar®. With some 250 films to his name, Friedhofer is only now becoming more appreciated as one of Hollywood's great composers.

Another refugee from Nazi-occupied Europe who found his way to Hollywood and studied with

Arnold Schoenberg in Los Angeles was **Franz Waxman**. Almost immediately, Waxman struck gold with *Bride of Frankenstein*.

At a glance: Franz Waxman

Born: 1906
Died: 1967
Must listen: *Bride of Frankenstein* (1935), *The Philadelphia Story* (1940), *Rebecca* (1940), *Alias Nick Beal* (1949), *Sunset Boulevard* (1950), *A Place in the Sun* (1951), *The Silver Chalice* (1955), *The Nun's Story* (1960), *Taras Bulba* (1962)

Waxman's strange and haunting score for *Bride of Frankenstein* was an enormous hit. Universal offered him a 2-year contract as music director, scoring more than 20 films a year, after which he moved on to MGM, Warner Brothers and Paramount. He worked with Alfred Hitchcock on four pictures and produced some of his best scores. Waxman won his two Oscars® for *Sunset Boulevard* and *A Place in the Sun*. He also wrote popular concert works including the "*Carmen Fantasy*" for violin and orchestra.

Hungarian born **Miklós Rózsa** was a graduate of the Leipzig Conservatory whose concert works were performed in Paris. Moving to London, his fellow Hungarian Alexander Korda commissioned him to start composing for films. He relocated to California in 1940 to complete *The Thief of Baghdad* and stayed for the rest of his life.

At a glance: Miklós Rózsa

Born: 1907

Died: 1995

Must listen: *The Four Feathers* (1939), *The Thief of Baghdad* (1940), *Jungle Book* (1942), *Double Indemnity* (1944), *Spellbound* (1945), *The Killers* (1946), *A Double Life* (1947), *Ben-Hur* (1959), *El Cid* (1961), *King of Kings* (1961), *The Private Life of Sherlock Holmes* (1970)

Rózsa composed music for more than 100 films, winning three Oscars® and another 14 nominations. His style ranges from the stridently epic and richly romantic of *Ben-Hur* to eerie *film noir* scores. *Spellbound*, for Hitchcock, employs the early electronic instrument, the theremin. Rózsa later adapted his score into a concert piece, the "*Spellbound Concerto*".

Bernard Herrmann owed his lucky break to Orson Welles, with whom he worked on radio. Welles commissioned Herrmann to provide the score for his first film – and masterpiece – *Citizen Kane*.

In *Citizen Kane*, Herrmann demonstrated that he could successfully tackle any style of music – from grand opera to jaunty humour. Later, he would apply his considerable talent to everything ranging from psychological thrillers to "sword and sorcery" adventures. But it is as much for his collaboration

At a glance: Bernard Herrmann

Born: 1911

Died: 1975

Must listen: *Citizen Kane* (1941), *The Devil and Daniel Webster* (1941), *The Magnificent Ambersons* (1942), *Anna and the King of Siam* (1946), *The Day the Earth Stood Still* (1951), *The Trouble with Harry* (1956), *Vertigo* (1958), *North by Northwest* (1959), *Psycho* (1960), *Taxi Driver* (1975)

with Alfred Hitchcock as his legendary irascibility that Herrmann is best remembered. He was a master when it came to creating a dark, brooding atmosphere. In *Psycho*, his screeching violins for the murder in the shower have inspired horror movie soundtracks to this day.

The commercial power of putting a good melody in a movie was first noticed properly when Fox Studios were inundated with requests after *Laura*. After Newman and Herrmann separately refused to score it, **David Raksin**'s theme became a huge hit with

At a glance: David Raksin

Born: 1912

Died: 2004

Must listen: *Laura* (1944), *Forever Amber* (1947), *Force of Evil* (1949), *The Bad and the Beautiful* (1952), *Separate Tables* (1959)

five different versions making it into the US Top 10. During Raksin's own lifetime, "*Laura*" was said to be the second most recorded song ever.

As early as 1936, Raksin – who lived into his 90s and became known as the "grandfather of film music" – had worked with Charles Chaplin on the score to *Modern Times*, with Chaplin thinking up the tunes and Raksin writing them down. Raksin was Oscar®-nominated for both *Forever Amber* and *Separate Tables*.

Most of Hollywood's Golden Age composers continued to work beyond the decade of the 1940s but, thanks to Bernard Herrmann, film music had broken free from its romantic European classical roots and became something altogether more individual, more supportive of the story – and less overwhelming.

Yet the style of Korngold, Newman, Waxman and the others has left its mark, particularly on the magnificent soundtracks of John Williams. Think *Star Wars*, *Indiana Jones*, *Schindler's List* and you'll realize the Golden Age never really ended.

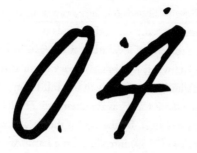

New Directions

The 1950s marked an era of innovation and
experimentation in cinema. As television began to
emerge as the dominant form of entertainment of
the decade, filmmakers had to employ the latest
technology to make things bigger and better to keep
the punters coming in. Epic movies still required
the likes of Alfred Newman and Miklós Rózsa to do
what they did best. But a revolution in the music
industry at the end of the 1940s – the introduction
of the long-playing record and the 7-inch single –
resulted in a change of attitude towards film. **Anton
Karas**'s "*Harry Lime Theme*", from *The Third Man*,
stayed at the top of the charts for almost 3 months
in 1950. This typically mid-European tune, played
on a zither by a hitherto unknown performer,

pioneered a new kind of musical authenticity in film scoring and signalled that the studios were willing to branch out and away from the grand romantic score into other kinds of music for films. The rock'n'roll revolution also began to make an impact when MGM's visionary music director Charles Wolcott chose to use Bill Haley's "*Rock around the Clock*" as the theme to *The Blackboard Jungle* (1955). By the end of the decade, *Black Orpheus* (1959) introduced the Latin American music styles of samba and bossa nova to a worldwide audience.

The value of using music to generate excitement about a film in advance of its release was also recognized when the song "*Do Not Forsake Me O My Darling*", which was an integral part of *High Noon* (1952), became a hit and served to promote the film. The formula was repeated in 1956 by its composer **Dmitri Tiomkin** with *Friendly Persuasion* and the song *"Thee I Love"*.

At a glance: Dmitri Tiomkin

Born:	1894
Died:	1979
Must listen:	*Lost Horizon* (1937), *Mr Smith Goes to Washington* (1939), *Duel in the Sun* (1946), *High Noon* (1952), *Friendly Persuasion* (1956), *Giant* (1956), *The Guns of Navarone* (1961), *The Fall of the Roman Empire* (1964)

Dmitri Tiomkin was a Ukrainian pianist who had given the European premiere of Gershwin's Piano Concerto in Paris in 1928. Tiomkin's wife, a choreographer, suggested they work on dance for the movies and together they devised ballet sequences for MGM. The composer's breakthrough came with *Lost Horizon* and its quasi-mystical sound world of chanting and percussion. Ironically for a Russian, Tiomkin made his biggest mark on that most American of genres – the western – with his expansive, folk-tinged scores. His triumphant music for *The Fall of the Roman Empire* is as big as Hollywood epic soundtracks ever got.

Tiomkin also contributed to the burgeoning sci-fi scene in the 1950s with a weird and wonderful score for *The Thing from Another World* (1951). Strange and unusual sounds entered soundtracks with the use of the theremin and other bleeping, electronically generated voices. Even Bernard Herrmann joined in the futuristic fun with one of his best scores, *The Day the Earth Stood Still* (1951), before moving on to more earth-based, but equally improbable, fantasies at the end of the decade, including *The Seventh Voyage of Sinbad* (1958) and *Jason and the Argonauts* (1963).

In Britain, the Ealing studios employed **Georges Auric** among others to bring wit and elegance to their distinctive comedies.

At a glance: Georges Auric

Born: 1899

Died: 1983

Must listen: *La belle et la bête* (1946), *Passport to Pimlico* (1949), *The Lavender Hill Mob* (1951), *Moulin Rouge* (1952), *Roman Holiday* (1953)

Auric was among the most outstanding composers of film music. Originally he was a member of Les Six, a circle of French composers who had gathered around the poet/playwright Jean Cocteau to produce a new kind of French music. Cocteau was keen to expand his cultural vision into film and began his collaboration with Auric on *La belle et la bête*. In addition to the work he produced for Ealing, Auric also scored a number of Hollywood romantic comedies.

With **Alex North**'s score to *A Streetcar named Desire*, jazz entered the vocabulary of film composers and movie music found a distinctly American voice.

At a glance: Alex North

Born: 1910

Died: 1991

Must listen: *A Streetcar named Desire* (1951), *Viva Zapata!* (1952), *The Bad Seed* (1956), *Spartacus* (1960), *The Misfits* (1961), *Who's Afraid of Virginia Woolf?* (1966)

A graduate of Juilliard, Alex North studied composition with Aaron Copland and wrote ballet scores and incidental music for the theatre. While *A Streetcar named Desire* launched a new era in film music, North's thrilling music for *Spartacus* nine years later is one of cinema's great epic soundtracks. It's a richly varied, inventively orchestrated score, shifting from the brassy and percussive, through to sweet romanticism. North went on to compose some of his most brilliant music for *2001: A Space Odyssey* (1968) but it was dropped when the director Stanley Kubrick decided to opt for a wholly classical score. North also had a huge international hit with his theme for *Unchained* (1955), better known as "*Unchained Melody*", later revived for *Ghost* (1990). Jerry Goldsmith said of North:

Of all of us, he's the master.

The introduction of jazz into film scores also launched the career of **Elmer Bernstein**, one of Hollywood's greatest masters of movie music.

At a glance: Elmer Bernstein

Born:	1922
Died:	2004
Must listen:	*The Man with the Golden Arm* (1955), *The Ten Commandments* (1956), *The Magnificent Seven* (1960), *To Kill a Mockingbird* (1962), *The Great Escape* (1963), *The Age of Innocence* (1993)

Bernstein, formerly a composer for the armed forces and a pianist, got his lucky break when he was called in to write the grand, exotic soundtrack for biblical epic *The Ten Commandments* after the death of Victor Young, who had previously been signed up to do it. But it was Bernstein's sparse, lyrical jazz score for *The Man with the Golden Arm* that made the bigger impact. A bestselling album, it helped producers to see the commercial value of recouping a movie's costs with a popular record. Bernstein's rollicking *The Magnificent Seven* theme and *The Great Escape* with its cheery march both became classics that have enjoyed a long, independent life in the concert hall, on disc and as favourites for military bands. His score for *To Kill a Mockingbird* is heart-warmingly simple and nostalgic. Bernstein continued to work tirelessly into his final years, as a conductor and composer of high-class scores, such as for Martin Scorsese's *The Age of Innocence*.

A former school friend of Bernard Herrmann's, **Jerome Moross** began his career in Hollywood as an orchestrator before establishing his name as a film composer with another blockbusting western, *The Big Country.*

Moross's first film scores for low-budget movies earned him sufficient money to fund his other career as a composer for the concert hall. With *The Big Country*, he perfected a rugged, expansive style that perfectly conjured up images of the American

> ## At a glance: Jerome Moross
> Born: 1913
> Died: 1983
> Must listen: *The Big Country* (1958), *The Adventures of Huckleberry Finn* (1960), *Five Finger Exercise* (1962), *The War Lord* (1965), *The Valley of Gwangi* (1968)

plains. In spite of considerable success, Moross saw his work for the movies as being of secondary importance to his "serious" compositions.

Leonard Rosenman, another film composer who studied composition under Arnold Schoenberg, was piano teacher to a young actor named James Dean, who gave Rosenman his lucky break.

> ## At a glance: Leonard Rosenman
> Born: 1924
> Died: 2008
> Must listen: *East of Eden* (1955), *Rebel without a Cause* (1955), *Fantastic Voyage* (1966), *The Lord of the Rings* (1978)

Dean introduced his music teacher to the director Elia Kazan, who invited him to score *East of Eden*. The romantic score, reminiscent of Samuel Barber's music, was a great success. However, Rosenman was not afraid to introduce elements of modernism into his music for the big screen. For *The Cobweb* (1955), he evoked the neuroses of patients in an asylum with a Schoenberg-style serialism played by a stark chamber orchestra. After a spell in Rome as a conductor, Rosenman returned to Hollywood to write avant-garde scores for *Fantastic Voyage* and *Beneath the Planet of the Apes* (1970). Rosenman's score for the original animated adaptation of *The Lord of the Rings* is an exceptional example of large scale symphonic and choral film scoring.

As many composers launched their careers in the mid-1950s in Hollywood with jazz, in Britain, the Hammer studios of low-budget horror films gave classically trained **James Bernard** his break.

At a glance: James Bernard

Born: 1925
Died: 2001
Must listen: *The Quatermass Experiment* (1955), *The Curse of Frankenstein* (1957), *Dracula* (1958), *She* (1965), *The Devil Rides Out* (1968)

James Bernard studied at the Royal College of Music and was an apprentice to Benjamin Britten. When an old RAF chum, John Hollingsworth, was appointed music director for Hammer, Bernard was brought in to provide the unnerving, atonal scores. He wrote the music for 23 Hammer horror features. In 1997, he came out of retirement to write a new score to the classic silent Dracula film, *Nosferatu* (1922).

A more modernist style also found its way into the music being written for films coming out of Scandinavia.

At a glance: Erik Nordgren

Born: 1913

Died: 1992

Must listen: *Secrets of Women* (1952), *The Seventh Seal* (1958), *Wild Strawberries* (1958), *The Pleasure Garden* (1961)

Erik Nordgren wrote music for some 40 films but it was his collaboration with Ingmar Bergman that signalled a change in the way that directors incorporated music into their work. The music is used sparingly, only to punctuate in short bursts rather than underscore a long sequence of action.

Throughout cinema's brief history, the retelling of classic stories – be they biblical, mythological or great works of literature – progressed side by side with filmmakers' reflecting on the concerns and issues of their own times. If the 1950s were the embodiment of youthful rebellion and challenging the past, the following decade saw Hollywood entering its jet-set era, opening up to a whole world of influences and styles.

05

Expanding Horizons

Cinemagoers' horizons in the late 1950s and early 1960s were expanded to accommodate the so-called "new wave" of films emerging from France. Among the Gallic composers who were lured across the pond to give Hollywood productions a continental flavour was **Georges Delerue**.

Delerue studied with Darius Milhaud at the Paris Conservatoire and composed for the theatre before writing jaunty, melodic scores for new wave filmmakers including François Truffaut, Alain Resnais and Jean-Luc Godard. Delerue wrote more than 200 film soundtracks while maintaining a

At a glance: Georges Delerue

Born: 1925

Died: 1992

Must listen: *Hiroshima mon amour* (1958), *Jules et Jim*
             (1962), *A Man for All Seasons* (1966), *Day
             for Night* (1973), *A Little Romance* (1979),
             Something Wicked This Way Comes (1983),
             Agnes of God (1985), *Platoon* (1986),
             Salvador (1986)

career composing for the concert hall. His excellent later scores for *Something Wicked This Way Comes* and *Platoon* were both rejected before the films were released but are well worth discovering.

Another French composer who successfully crossed the pond to Hollywood was **Francis Lai**.

At a glance: Francis Lai

Born: 1932

Must listen: *Un homme et une femme* (1965), *Live for
             Life* (1967), *Mayerling* (1968), *Love Story*
             (1970)

Francis Lai's big breakthrough came with the Oscar®-nominated theme to *Un homme et une femme,* a Cannes Palme d'Or winner. The iconic easy listening-style theme took up residence in the US pop charts for almost two years. Lai's career flourished in his native France, as well as in Britain

and America, peaking when he received an Oscar®
in 1970 for *Love Story*.

Lai's exact contemporary **Michel Legrand** began his
career as a conductor and arranger for Maurice
Chevalier and Jacques Brel.

At a glance: Michel Legrand

Born: 1932
Must listen: *Les parapluies de Cherbourg* (1964),
               Ice Station Zebra (1968), *The Thomas
               Crown Affair* (1968), *Summer of '42*
               (1971)

Nine years after his first film score, Legrand's
breakthough came with the song "*I will Wait
for You*" from *Les parapluies de Cherbourg*
(*The Umbrellas of Cherbourg*). Legrand's
move to Hollywood in 1968 led to further
success, particularly with the song "*The
Windmills of Your Mind*", from *The Thomas
Crown Affair*.

At a glance: Maurice Jarre

Born: 1924
Died: 2009
Must listen: *Lawrence of Arabia* (1962), *Doctor Zhivago*
               (1965), *The Year of Living Dangerously*
               (1982), *A Passage to India* (1984), *Witness*
               (1985), *Ghost* (1990)

Of all the French composers who emerged in the 1960s, **Maurice Jarre** created the scores that are the most internationally recognizable and enduring.

Throughout the 1950s, Jarre collaborated with the director Georges Franju, writing a number of avant-garde soundtracks. In 1962, Jarre was approached to compose the music to David Lean's epic *Lawrence of Arabia* after attempts to sign up Malcolm Arnold, William Walton, Benjamin Britten and Aram Khachaturian had failed. Jarre completed the magnificent music in just four weeks and won an Oscar®. A legendary partnership with Lean was born, which resulted in Jarre winning further Oscars® for *Dr Zhivago* and *A Passage to India*.

Emerging from Italy, **Nino Rota** became one of the most prolific of all film composers with almost 150 scores to his name, as well as ballets, operas, choral and chamber works.

At a glance: Nino Rota

Born:	1911
Died:	1979
Must listen:	*The Glass Mountain* (1949), *La Dolce Vita* (1959), *The Leopard* (1963), *Romeo and Juliet* (1968), *The Godfather* (1972), *Orchestra Rehearsal* (1978)

Rota's longstanding partnership with the director
Federico Fellini began with *The White Sheik* (1952)
and lasted through to Fellini's last film, *Orchestra
Rehearsal.* Rota's theme from Franco Zeffirelli's
Romeo and Juliet was a number 1 hit and heard
daily on UK radio for more than a decade when
Classic FM's Simon Bates used it to underscore his
weekday "*Our Tune*" feature on BBC Radio 1.
Rota's most famous work is the traditional-style
score he composed for *The Godfather.* Its love
theme, with lyrics added, became the worldwide hit
"*Speak Softly Love*". Rota won a posthumous Oscar®
for its sequel, *The Godfather II.*

A movie music legend – also Italian – emerged in
the 1960s and has continued to produce masterful
scores into the 21st century – **Ennio Morricone**.

At a glance: Ennio Morricone

Born: 1928

Must listen: *A Fistful of Dollars* (1964), *The Good, the
Bad and the Ugly* (1966), *Once upon a Time
in the West* (1968), *Once Upon a Time in
America* (1984), *The Mission* (1986), *The
Untouchables* (1987), *Cinema Paradiso*
(1989), *The Legend of 1900* (1998), *Malena*
(2000)

Morricone has always considered himself a composer
of concert music who writes for films on the side, so
to speak. Yet his extensive, magnificent output has

placed him firmly in the Pantheon of great film composers. Morricone's name will forever be linked with the director Sergio Leone, with whom he first collaborated on *A Fistful of Dollars* and subsequent "spaghetti westerns". The film reinvented the western genre. Morricone's sound palette of coyote howls, whistles, whips, harmonicas, electric guitars and lyricless vocals established him as a true original in film music. For Classic FM listeners, Morricone's most popular score is *The Mission*, which merges tribal Amazonian rhythms with the baroque style exported by Jesuit missionaries to South America in the 18th century.

The Mediterranean region also gave 1960s film music its only Greek superstar, **Mikis Theodorakis**.

At a glance: Mikis Theodorakis

Born: 1925

Must listen: *Phaedra* (1962), *Zorba the Greek* (1964), *Z* (1969), *Serpico* (1973)

Theodorakis, who studied with Olivier Messiaen at the Paris Conservatoire, initially achieved success writing ballet music for Rudolf Nureyev and Margot Fonteyn. Turning his attention to Greek pop music and the cinema, Theodorakis had an international hit with his theme to *Zorba the Greek*. His own revolutionary ideas and attacks on Greece's then military regime resulted in his music being banned, then his own imprisonment and subsequent exile.

One of Hollywood's all-time masters of movie music
emerged in the 1960s and continued on magnificent
form for four decades – **Jerry Goldsmith.**

At a glance: Jerry Goldsmith

Born: 1929

Died: 2004

Must listen: *The Blue Max* (1966), *Planet of the Apes*
             (1968), *Patton* (1970), *The Omen* (1976),
             Alien (1979), *Poltergeist* (1982), *First Knight*
             (1995), *LA Confidential* (1997)

Goldsmith attended classes given by Miklós Rózsa
at the University of Southern California before
getting work as a clerk in the music department of
CBS. Composing work for television and radio
dramas followed, where Goldsmith built his
reputation providing the music for series such as
Gunsmoke and *The Twilight Zone*. His compositions
– which spanned every kind of film genre – often
showed off an adventurous spirit, one willing to
experiment with unusual sounds and technology. In
his soundtrack for *Planet of the Apes*, Goldsmith
incorporated all manner of percussion including
household utensils and rams' horns.

Goldsmith won his only Oscar® for the sinister,
choral soundtrack to *The Omen*. For *First Knight*,
one of his best later scores, he paid brilliant homage
to the Golden Age of Hollywood epics and the
music of Rózsa and Newman.

Enrico Nicola Mancini – better known as **Henry Mancini** – was one of the most influential and successful film composers in the 1960s.

At a glance: Henry Mancini

Born: 1924
Died: 1994
Must listen: *Touch of Evil* (1958), *Breakfast at Tiffany's* (1961), *Hatari!* (1962), *Charade* (1963), *The Pink Panther* (1964), *The Great Race* (1965), *The Molly Maguires* (1970), *Lifeforce* (1985)

Henry Mancini was never a film composer in the grand symphonic style. Much of his music is quintessentially of its time – swinging, light and frivolous. The popularity of the ballad, "*Moon River*" from *Breakfast at Tiffany's* meant that Mancini was expected to deliver chart hits with every one of his film scores. With *The Pink Panther*'s jazzy saxophone theme and *Hatari!*'s boogie-woogie "*Baby Elephant Walk*", Mancini's enduring contribution to film music was his notion that the soundtrack should be clearly heard and not demoted to providing subliminal emotional cues. Mancini paved the way for the likes of Lalo Schifrin, Burt Bacharach and **John Barry** to create scores that were stylistically inseparable from the pop music of their day.

Barry started out with his own jazz combo – the John Barry Seven – working closely with pop star

At a glance: John Barry

Born: 1933

Must listen: *From Russia with Love* (1963), *Zulu* (1964),
            Born Free (1965), *The Lion in Winter* (1968),
            Walkabout (1970), *Robin and Marian* (1976),
            Somewhere in Time (1980), *Out of Africa*
            (1985), *Dances with Wolves* (1990)

Adam Faith. Barry was asked to arrange the music
for Faith's film *Beat Girl* (1959) before working on
James Bond's first outing in *Dr No* (1962). The
composer of the original James Bond theme was
Monty Norman. Ten Bond scores by Barry followed
in which he made his indelible mark on the Bond
sound. Barry's Bond songs resulted in numerous
chart hits, as did his Oscar®-winning *Born Free*
score. More Oscars® followed for *The Lion in
Winter*, *Out of Africa* and *Dances with Wolves*. In the
main themes for the last two, Barry reached the
peak of his powers, demonstrating an enduring gift
for sweeping, romantic melodies.

The 1960s and 1970s were also eras in which
directors increasingly incorporated classical music
into their soundtracks, bringing works that
previously had mainly been enjoyed by concertgoers
to worldwide audiences.

The Swedish film *Elvira Madigan* (1967) gave
Mozart's Piano Concerto No. 21 a new lease of life

and a subtitle by which it has been known ever since. The release of *2001: A Space Odyssey* the following year, coinciding as it did with the global excitement at America and Russia's space programmes, made the "*Sunrise*" opening to Richard Strauss's *Also Sprach Zarathustra* an often heard anthem for the space age, as well as grand sporting occasions. The soundtrack album to *2001* was a great commercial success. Director Stanley Kubrick would later also turn to works from the classical repertoire in his soundtrack choices for *A Clockwork Orange* (1971) and *The Shining* (1980).

Luchino Visconti's languorous 1971 adaptation of *Death in Venice*, starring Dirk Bogarde as a dying composer – loosely based on Gustav Mahler – made exceptional use of the heart-rending *Adagietto* movement of Mahler's own Symphony No. 5.

The increased use of classical music in movies of this period was welcome, in view of the dearth of good new film scores being composed.

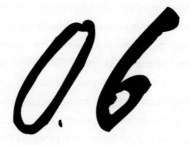

May the Force be With You!

Orchestral film music at the beginning of the 1970s was in the doldrums. It was American urban funk music that made the biggest impact on the soundtracks of the era with Isaac Hayes' *Shaft*, the precursor to disco domination towards the end of the decade with the huge success of *Saturday Night Fever* (1977). Throughout the early 1970s, Jerry Goldsmith kept the flag flying for the composed, original score and delivered superlative soundtracks for the likes of *The Mephisto Waltz* (1972), *Tora! Tora! Tora!* (1970) and *The Other* (1972).

It was thanks, however, to the public's seemingly insatiable appetite for disaster movies that a talent emerged mid-decade who has become the most successful movie composer of all time – **John Williams**.

At a glance: John Williams

Born: 1932

Must listen: *The Towering Inferno* (1974), *Jaws* (1975), *Close Encounters of the Third Kind* (1977), *Star Wars* (1977), *Superman: The Movie* (1978), *The Empire Strikes Back* (1980), *Raiders of the Lost Ark* (1981), *ET: The Extra-Terrestrial* (1982), *Empire of the Sun* (1987), *Born on the Fourth of July* (1989), *Jurassic Park* (1993), *Schindler's List* (1994), *Amistad* (1997), *Seven Years in Tibet* (1997), *Saving Private Ryan* (1998), *Angela's Ashes* (1999), *Harry Potter and the Philosopher's Stone* (2001), *Catch Me if You Can* (2002), *Minority Report* (2002), *The Terminal* (2004), *Memoirs of a Geisha* (2005), *Munich* (2005)

Williams trained as a concert pianist before conducting bands in the US Air Force. He took composition lessons from Mario Castelnuovo-Tedesco, who had also taught Jerry Goldsmith. As a pianist, Williams worked for Alfred Newman, Franz Waxman and Dimitri Tiomkin – and provided the piano part in Henry Mancini's *Peter Gunn* television theme – before taking up composing for TV series including *Wagon Train* and *Lost in Space*. The demands of delivering up to one hour of music a week honed his craft as a composer, although Williams' first Oscar® was awarded in 1971 for his adaptation of the stage show *Fiddler on the Roof*. High-profile work on disaster movies followed, including *Earthquake* (1974), *The Poseidon Adventure* (1972) and *The Towering Inferno* (1974).

Williams' collaboration with director Steven Spielberg began in 1974 with *The Sugarland Express*. Their partnership has given the world not only some of its biggest box office smashes, but some of the best loved film themes of all time – music that exists in its own right outside of the films as favourites in the concert hall, on CD and on Classic FM.

Star Wars – all brassy fanfares and Holstian marches – was the one soundtrack that single-handedly revived the tradition of the big orchestral film score. On disc, it became the biggest selling non-pop record ever. Along with *Raiders of the Lost Ark* and *Superman*, it recalls the Golden Age of Korngold, Rózsa and Steiner. For *Schindler's List, Born on the Fourth of July* and *Saving Private Ryan*, Williams has penned some of the most emotionally stirring orchestral music of the late 20th century.

John Williams is the most Oscar®-nominated person ever – with more than 40 nominations and four wins for his own compositions – *Jaws, Star Wars, ET* and *Schindler's List.* With more music currently in the pipeline for Spielberg – *Tintin* and a biopic of Abraham Lincoln – it seems that John Williams, now in his 70s, is simply unstoppable.

While John Williams and the spate of *Star Wars*-spawned sci-fi blockbusters revived film music's grand orchestral tradition, a Greek pop musician was revolutionizing the use of electronics on soundtracks.

At a glance: Vangelis

Born: 1943

Must listen: *Chariots of Fire* (1981), *Blade Runner* (1982), *Missing* (1982), *1492: Conquest of Paradise* (1992), *Alexander* (2004)

Vangelis Odysseas Papathanassiou enjoyed pop chart success as a member of the band Aphrodite's Child with Demis Roussos. For *Chariots of Fire*, a period piece about British Olympic athletes, Vangelis's brand of synthesizer-generated music was an unusual choice. But the gamble paid off – *Chariots* was a runaway international hit, as a film and a soundtrack, and Vangelis went on to provide atmospheric scores for numerous other films including the futuristic cult classic, *Blade Runner*.

Another international synthesiser wizard who made the move to soundtracks from the world of pop was **Ryuichi Sakamoto**.

At a glance: Ryuichi Sakamoto

Born: 1952

Must listen: *Merry Christmas, Mr Lawrence* (1983), *The Last Emperor* (1987), *The Sheltering Sky* (1991), *Little Buddha* (1993), *Babel* (2007), *Silk* (2007)

Sakamoto was a founding member of the Japanese electronic pop group Yellow Magic Orchestra. He not only scored *Merry Christmas, Mr Lawrence*, but also starred in it alongside David Bowie. Its catchy oriental theme became a chart hit as "*Forbidden Colours*", sung by David Sylvian. Sakamoto received an Oscar® with Talking Heads frontman David Byrne for Bertolucci's epic, *The Last Emperor*. He has produced atmospheric, piano-based scores for a number of Japanese films as well as contributing to the Oscar®-winning soundtrack for *Babel*.

James Horner is a hugely successful film composer who, riding on the wave of science-fiction epics, hit gold with the second big screen outing for Captain Kirk and the crew of the USS *Enterprise*.

American born but educated at London's Royal College of Music, Horner set out to be an avant-

At a glance: James Horner

Born: 1953

Must listen: *Star Trek II: The Wrath of Khan* (1982),
             Apollo 13 (1985), *Cocoon* (1985), *Aliens*
             (1986), *Field of Dreams* (1989), *Glory*
             (1989), *Braveheart* (1995), *Titanic* (1997),
             Mighty Joe Young (1998), *A Beautiful Mind*
             (2001), *Enemy at the Gates* (2001), *Iris*
             (2001), *The Four Feathers* (2002), *Troy*
             (2004), *Apocalypto* (2006), *The Boy in the
             Striped Pyjamas* (2008)

garde composer for the concert hall but soon caught
the film music bug, writing music for science-
fiction B movies produced by Roger Corman's
company New World. There he met young directors
who would become close collaborators – notably
Ron Howard and James Cameron. After *Star Trek
II: The Wrath of Khan*, Horner was nominated for
an Oscar® for *Aliens*, directed by Cameron. The two
reunited for *Titanic*, spawning a global
phenomenon and a smash hit single – Céline Dion's
"*My Heart Will Go On*". Horner's scores – including
Braveheart and *Titanic* – have often made effective
use of unusual traditional instruments, such as
bagpipes and whistles. He continues to compose
evocative scores, though nothing has surpassed his
blockbusting form of the late 1990s. For *Troy*,
Horner stepped in a few weeks before the film's
premiere when the director decided to ditch the

music that Gabriel Yared had spent a year working on. In a month, Horner produced a magnificent epic score that recalls the best of Rózsa and Korngold.

A fluency in both pop and classical styles characterized the music of **Michael Kamen**.

At a glance: Michael Kamen

Born: 1948

Died: 2003

Must listen: *The Dead Zone* (1983), *Brazil* (1985), *Highlander* (1986), *Die Hard* (1988), *Robin Hood, Prince of Thieves* (1991), *Don Juan de Marco* (1995), *Mr Holland's Opus* (1995), *X-Men* (2000)

Michael Kamen's CV read like a rollcall of pop royalty. He worked with Kate Bush, The Eurythmics, Pink Floyd, Bob Dylan and Eric Clapton, to name but a few. Kamen's first major film assignment was scoring David Cronenberg's *The Dead Zone*. Working with *Monty Python*'s Terry Gilliam on *Brazil* brought out the best in Kamen. The soundtrack is one of the movie music masterpieces of the 1980s. His Bryan Adams-sung theme for *Robin Hood, Prince of Thieves*, "*Everything I Do*", topped the UK charts for no fewer than 16 weeks in 1991, demonstrating once again the power of a good film tune to generate audiences, revenue and excitement about going to the cinema.

From the Nineties to the Noughties

At the end of the 1980s, one composer emerged on the movie scene whose sound – and influence – dominated film music for the 1990s and, by now, for much of the first decade of the 21st century. Just as Hollywood's composers in the 1950s brought jazz into the vocabulary of film music, **Hans Zimmer** has successfully blended conventional orchestral and choral forces with rock elements, including synthesizers and electronic drums, to create a thrilling, contemporary sound.

At a glance: Hans Zimmer

Born: 1957

Must listen: *Rain Man* (1988), *Black Rain* (1989),
             Backdraft (1991), *The Power of One* (1992),
             The Lion King (1993), *Beyond Rangoon*
             (1994), *The Prince of Egypt* (1998),
             Gladiator (2000), *Black Hawk Down* (2001),
             Spirit: Stallion of the Cimarron (2002), *The
             Last Samurai* (2003), *King Arthur* (2004),
             Batman Begins (2005, with James Newton
             Howard), *The Da Vinci Code* (2006), *Pirates
             of the Caribbean: Dead Man's Chest* (2006),
             The Dark Knight (2008, with James Newton
             Howard)

German-born Zimmer began his musical career
working with rock bands including The Damned,
Ultravox and The Buggles. As an apprentice to
English film composer Stanley Myers, Zimmer
contributed music to a number of movies in the
mid–1980s including Daniel Day Lewis's *My
Beautiful Laundrette* (1985).

Zimmer's big break came with an invitation from
director Barry Levinson to score *Rain Man*, starring
Tom Cruise and Dustin Hoffman. His soundtrack
to Ridley Scott's *Black Rain* was a milestone,
featuring the composer's now familiar mix of
computer-generated sounds, electronic percussion
and orchestra and casting the mould for almost

every action feature in the decade to follow. Zimmer won his first Oscar® for Disney's *The Lion King*, in which he seamlessly blended large orchestral forces with the African choral music of Lebo M and Elton John's songs.

Zimmer's collaboration with Lisa Gerrard on Ridley Scott's *Gladiator* resulted in a worldwide, bestselling CD. The composer and the director have also worked together on *Thelma and Louise* (1991), *Black Hawk Down* (2001), *Hannibal* (2001) and *Matchstick Men* (2003).

Another major contribution that Zimmer has made to the craft of movie music was his establishment of Media Ventures, more recently called Remote Control Productions, a studio complex that provides a creative environment for several film composers to work in. The project offers producers a one-stop shop for their musical requirements and many of today's busiest film composers – among them Mark Mancina, John Powell, Trevor Rabin, Klaus Badelt and Harry Gregson-Williams – have started out by collaborating with Zimmer on his blockbusters. In a move echoing the old-style Hollywood studios' employing composers to manage their in-house music departments, Zimmer was made music supervisor to Dreamworks SKG, an appointment that has ensured his involvement in some of the most successful entertainment movies of the recent past.

The partnership between Ridley Scott and Hans Zimmer is continuing a long tradition in which directors and composers enjoy a successful working relationship – think Hitchcock and Herrmann, Lean and Jarre, Fellini and Rota, Bergman and Nordgren, Spielberg and Williams. This close collaboration – which often brings out the best in both the director and composer – has continued in recent times with a number of highly creative partnerships.

Howard Shore owes his initial success to the Canadian master of shock horror, David Cronenberg, and his worldwide fame to New Zealand's very own *Lord of the Rings*, Peter Jackson.

At a glance: Howard Shore

Born:	1946
Must listen:	*The Fly* (1986), *Silence of the Lambs* (1990), *Se7en* (1995), *Looking for Richard* (1996), *The Lord of the Rings* trilogy (2001–2003), *The Aviator* (2004), *Eastern Promises* (2007)

Toronto-born Shore toured with rock bands and wrote incidental music for theatre and radio before landing the music director's job on US television's popular *Saturday Night Live*. His collaboration with David Cronenberg began with *The Brood* (1979) and has continued for 30 years, up to and including Cronenberg's more recent, mainstream – but equally bloody – thrillers, such as *A History of*

Violence. For Cronenberg, Shore provided one of his grandest early achievements, *The Fly*, which he has now turned into an opera that has been staged in Paris and the USA.

Shore's work with Cronenberg prepared him well for other spine-chilling excursions – including, for Ridley Scott, a sparse, atmospheric and genre-setting score for *Silence of the Lambs* and, for David Fincher, unsettling music for *The Game* (1997) and *Se7en*.

The three, monumental *Lord of the Rings* soundtracks firmly established Shore as an A-list Hollywood composer and dominated CD charts all over the world. A foretaste of his talent for marshalling orchestral and choral elements can be heard in his exquisite music for Al Pacino's Shakespeare documentary, *Looking for Richard.* For *Lord of the Rings*, Shore pulled out all the stops, brought in world-class soloists and singers and created a contemporary classical masterpiece, now performed to sold-out concert halls and voted by Classic FM listeners as their all-time favourite soundtrack.

Another distinctive, and devoted, director–composer partnership is the one enjoyed by Tim Burton and **Danny Elfman**.

Tim Burton first encountered Danny Elfman when the composer was playing with his rock band, Oingo Boingo. The two discovered they had a

At a glance: Danny Elfman

Born: 1949

Must listen: *Pee-Wee's Big Adventure* (1985), *Beetlejuice* (1988), *Batman* (1989), *Edward Scissorhands* (1990), *Batman Returns* (1992), *Mars Attacks!* (1996), *Good Will Hunting* (1997), *Men in Black* (1997), *Spiderman* (2002), *Big Fish* (2003), *Charlotte's Web* (2006), *The Wolf Man* (2009)

natural chemistry and between them created a trademark fantasy world with Elfman's off-beat, manic, musical wit and swirling fairytale orchestration perfectly matching Burton's skewed artistic vision. Their partnership gave the superhero genre an unusual twist with *Batman* and *Batman Returns* and has continued with quirky remakes of *Sleepy Hollow* (1997), *Charlie and the Chocolate Factory* (2005) and, coming to a screen near you soon, *Alice in Wonderland*. Elfman's most universally familiar work to date, however, has been for the small screen – the theme tune to *The Simpsons*.

A longstanding collaboration with director David Lynch on some of the most bizarre films of our time have won the composer **Angelo Badalamenti** critical acclaim.

New Yorker Badalamenti, born Andy Badale, won international recognition for Lynch's *Blue Velvet* and continued his partnership with the director on films

> ## At a glance: Angelo Badalamenti
> Born: 1937
>
> Must listen: *Blue Velvet* (1986), *City of Lost Children* (1995), *The Straight Story* (1999), *The Beach* (2000), *The Edge of Love* (2008)

such as *Lost Highway* (1997), *The Straight Story*, *Mulholland Drive* (2001) and the television series, *Twin Peaks*. Badalamenti's experimental style is an unnerving mixture of jazz, cabaret music, rock and elements of Bernard Herrmann at his most out of kilter.

Great British talent

In Britain, Scottish composer **Patrick Doyle** enjoyed the unique position of being part of the repertory company of creative talents that put Kenneth Branagh, Emma Thompson and their friends at the forefront of British theatre and cinema in the 1990s.

> ## At a glance: Patrick Doyle
> Born: 1953
>
> Must listen: *Henry V* (1989), *Carlito's Way* (1993), *Much Ado About Nothing* (1993), *A Little Princess* (1995), *Sense and Sensibility* (1995), *Hamlet* (1996), *Gosford Park* (2001), *Harry Potter and the Goblet of Fire* (2005)

Patrick Doyle joined Branagh's Renaissance Theatre
Company as an actor, composer and musical director
in 1987. His score for Branagh's *Henry V*, featuring
the stirring chorus "*Non Nobis Domini*", was a
triumph. It led to further collaborations on several
Shakespeare productions as well as a thriller – *Dead
Again* (1991) – and a terrifying score for an otherwise
unremarkable *Frankenstein* (1994). Doyle's sunny,
life-affirming score for *Much Ado About Nothing* is
one of the greatest soundtracks of the 1990s. His
pastiche Mozartian music for Emma Thompson's
production of *Sense and Sensibility* enjoyed a long run
in the Classic FM chart in the mid–1990s.

Another British composer who has successfully
cracked Hollywood is Luton-born **David Arnold**.

At a glance: David Arnold

Born: 1962

Must listen: *Stargate* (1994), *Independence Day* (1996), *Die
Another Day* (2002), *Casino Royale* (2007)

David Arnold's big break on the sci-fi film *Stargate*
led to the over-the-top bombast of *Independence
Day* and Arnold taking on John Barry's mantle as
James Bond's composer in residence. Starting with
Tomorrow Never Dies, Arnold has scored five Bond
outings and has made the sound his own – building
on Barry's legacy and introducing elements of rock,
"drum and bass" and high-tech pyrotechnics into
his highly accomplished soundtracks.

What about the women?

For reasons that are probably too complex to cover adequately here, film music in Hollywood has never been the preserve of women. In recent years, however, British women composers have made inroads into the male stronghold: **Debbie Wiseman** (1963–), whose bittersweet score for *Wilde* (1997) evoked the trials of the Victorian era's most controversial aesthete; **Rachel Portman** (1960–), who won an Oscar® in 1996 for *Emma*; **Anne Dudley** (1956–), whose soundtrack for *The Full Monty* (1997) picked up an Academy Award® the following year; Blackpool-born **Ilona Sekacz** (1948–), who won acclaim for her music for the Oscar®-winning *Antonia's Line* (1995); and **Jocelyn Pook** (1960–), who provided atmospheric music for Stanley Kubrick's final film *Eyes Wide Shut* (1999) and Martin Scorsese's *Gangs of New York* (2002). Australian born **Lisa Gerrard** (1961–) made a haunting vocal contribution to the *Gladiator* (2000) soundtrack and, two years later, provided a mysterious, atmospheric score for *Whale Rider* (2002).

More modern masters of movie music

The influence of film legend Alfred Newman has continued into our own time, with his sons Thomas and David and nephew Randy all enjoying successful careers as movie composers and making their mark on modern-day Hollywood.

At a glance: Thomas Newman

Born: 1955

Must listen: *Little Women* (1994), *The Shawshank Redemption* (1994), *American Beauty* (1999), *Road to Perdition* (2002), *Finding Nemo* (2003), *Cinderella Man* (2005), *WALL*E* (2008)

Thomas Newman studied with David Raksin at the University of Southern California. His early successes were synthesizer-based scores for *Reckless* (1984), *Desperately Seeking Susan* (1985) and *The Lost Boys* (1987). Two of his scores in 1994, *The Shawshank Redemption* and *Little Women*, were both Oscar® nominated. Newman's music flits between two styles – a quintessentially American symphonic sentimentality and a sparse, chilling minimalist style with reverberating piano and strange percussion, as heard on *American Beauty*. The latter style has been influential on Hollywood's younger composers and has even translated well into Pixar's recent animated masterpieces.

Classically trained **James Newton Howard** has moved into movies after years as a session musician, pianist, producer and arranger for the likes of Elton John, Cher and Chaka Khan. Howard has enjoyed strong director–composer relationships with Kevin Costner – working on *Wyatt Earp* (1994), *Waterworld* (1995) and *The Postman* (1997) – and

At a glance: James Newton Howard

Born: 1951

Must listen: *The Prince of Tides* (1991), *The Fugitive* (1993), *The Sixth Sense* (1999), *Snow Falling on Cedars* (1999), *Signs* (2002), *Peter Pan* (2003), *King Kong* (2005), *Batman Begins* (2006, with Hans Zimmer), *Blood Diamond* (2006), *I am Legend* (2007), *The Dark Knight* (2008, with Hans Zimmer)

director M. Night Shyamalan for whom he has created bleak, Herrmannesque soundtracks including *The Sixth Sense*. The two recent collaborations with Hans Zimmer on the revitalized *Batman* franchise are among Howard's finest work.

Elliot Goldenthal's soundtracks are characterized by a symphonic weight that reveals his classical music roots.

At a glance: Elliot Goldenthal

Born: 1954

Must listen: *Alien³* (1992), *Interview with the Vampire* (1993), *Michael Collins* (1996), *Titus* (1999), *Final Fantasy: The Spirits Within* (2001), *Frida* (2002)

Goldenthal first came to the public's attention with the music he wrote for the third film in the *Alien* franchise, followed by the sweeping gothic romanticism of *Interview with the Vampire*.

Goldenthal has collaborated often with his wife, the director Julie Taymor – who was responsible for *The Lion King* on stage. His Oscar®-winning soundtrack for *Frida* was an immaculately produced, Latin-style guitar score.

International newcomers

Some of the biggest names in contemporary film music are neither American nor British. Lebanese-born composer **Gabriel Yared** took home one of the nine Oscars® that went to Anthony Minghella's *The English Patient*.

At a glance: Gabriel Yared	
Born:	1949
Must listen:	*Betty Blue* (1986), *The Lover* (1992), *The English Patient* (1996), *The Talented Mr Ripley* (1999), *Possession* (2002), *Cold Mountain* (2003)

Yared left the Lebanon for Brazil, later moving to Paris. There he studied composition with the composer Henri Dutilleux and worked as a composer and arranger for numerous French recording artists, including Charles Aznavour. He spent much of the 1980s and 1990s writing for European films before composing the unassuming, at times John Barryesque, music for *The English Patient*, which was one of the decade's bestselling soundtracks.

An Argentinian who has become one of the biggest names in Hollywood, winning two Oscars® in successive years, is **Gustavo Santaolalla**.

At a glance: Gustavo Santaolalla

Born: 1951

Must listen: *The Motorcycle Diaries* (2004), *Brokeback Mountain* (2005), *Babel* (2006)

Santaolalla was a prominent figure on the Argentinian music scene for 3 decades before producing albums for Latin musicians in Los Angeles. His breakthrough into film composition came with *Amores Perros* (2000). Santaolalla's music for *Brokeback Mountain* beat off strong competition in the 2005 Oscars®, including two John Williams scores – for *Munich* and *Memoirs of a Geisha*. His success was consolidated the following year when he took another Best Original Score Oscar® for *Babel*, directed by his friend Alejandro González Iñárritu.

Another international composer who is making an impact on contemporary movie music is **Dario Marianelli**.

At a glance: Dario Marianelli

Born: 1963

Must listen: *I Capture the Castle* (2003), *Pride and Prejudice* (2005), *V for Vendetta* (2005), *Atonement* (2007)

Italian-born Marianelli's star rose quickly after he scored the Keira Knightley vehicle *Pride and Prejudice*, featuring exquisite piano music performed by the French pianist Jean-Yves Thibaudet. *Atonement*, also featuring Thibaudet (and also starring Knightley), took the Oscar® in 2007.

The arrival on the movie scene in recent years of talented young composers from various parts of the world, effortlessly bringing to soundtracks an understanding of many diverse genres of music, bodes well for the future of film music, still an art form that is barely a century old.

As John Williams says:

The process has really only begun. What's happened the last five or six decades has only been setting up a preparation, and a keen interest, and an awareness of the great musical opportunity that's here. It's an art form that's in its infancy. That's what's exciting.

The Classics at the Movies

Classical composers and their movie scores

As we learned back at the beginning of our *Friendly Guide*, some of the earliest filmmakers were eager to get composers involved in writing music for the screen and it was Camille Saint-Saëns who, in 1908, was commissioned to write the music for *L'Assassinat du Duc de Guise*. Maybe because of the considerable expense added to the budget of a film by hiring a composer to provide a score, the idea didn't take off immediately. But by the late 1920s and the arrival of sound films, composers were not

only in great demand, they relished the opportunity to earn much needed cash from providing music for the movies.

The Russians

In Russia, the young **Dmitry Shostakovich** worked as an improvising pianist in the cinema. He was sacked for laughing so much during one comedy that he forgot to play.

At a glance: Dmitry Shostakovich

Born: 1906

Died: 1975

Must listen: *The New Babylon* (1929), *Alone* (1931), *The Gadfly* (1955), *The Unforgettable Year 1919* (1952)

In 1929, Shostakovich was commissioned to write the score for *The New Babylon* and pioneered the music for Russia's first sound films. The *New Babylon* soundtrack is full of references to other pieces, including the "*Marseillaise*" and Offenbach's "*Can-Can*". In total, Shostakovich scored more than 30 films. At several points in his life, film work was all Shostakovich could get and he had no choice but to provide music for Communist propaganda films. For *The Unforgettable Year 1919*, Shostakovich composed "*The Assault on Beautiful Gorky*", a Rachmaninov-style piano work to rival Addinsell's "*Warsaw Concerto*". *The Gadfly* included the haunting "*Romance*", later made popular as the theme tune to the TV series, *Reilly, Ace of Spies*.

In 1933, another great Russian composer, **Sergei Prokofiev**, was approached to do his first film score.

At a glance: Sergei Prokofiev

Born: 1891

Died: 1953

Must listen: *Lieutenant Kijé* (1934), *Alexander Nevsky* (1939), *Lermontov* (1943), *Ivan the Terrible* (1942/1946)

Prokofiev completed his soundtrack for *Lieutenant Kijé* quickly and it was recorded in a Leningrad studio. While the film has been forgotten, the suite that Prokofiev put together – including the Christmassy *Troika* – has remained a favourite. For *Alexander Nevsky*, Prokofiev studied 12th- and 13th-century church music to try to create an authentic sound for the film but decided that a contemporary approach would suit the action better. *Nevsky*'s director, Sergei Eisenstein, described Prokofiev as "a perfect composer for the screen".

Prokofiev also took an active interest in the recording of the score, preferring to stay in the engineer's booth to hear the work through loudspeakers while someone else conducted it. He also later rearranged the music as a powerful cantata for mezzo-soprano, chorus and orchestra.

Prokofiev worked with Eisenstein again on *Ivan the Terrible* and, such was the chemistry between the director and composer, he turned down any more major film offers after Eisenstein's death.

The French

In France, composer **Arthur Honegger** was at his most prolific in the years between the two world wars.

At a glance: Arthur Honegger	
Born:	1892
Died:	1955
Must listen:	*Napoleon* (1927), *Les Misérables* (1934), *Mayerling* (1936), *Pygmalion* (1938), *Mermoz* (1942), *Pacific 231* (1946)

Honegger wrote more than 40 film scores, starting out with music written for Abel Gance's *La roue* (1923), which made use of musical effects suggesting the rhythm of railways – a technique he later used in his popular concert piece, *Pacific 231*. Honegger was a master at creating intense drama through his music and was never afraid to experiment. He even ventured into the world of animation with *L'idée* (1932), in which he made use of an early electronic instrument invented by Maurice Martenot and used most notably by fellow French composer Olivier

Messiaen, the Ondes Martenot. Honegger was also responsible for planting a seed in the mind of Miklós Rózsa to write music for films. Originally dismissive of the genre, Rózsa changed his mind – and career – after seeing *Napoleon* with Honegger's score.

Jacques Ibert also wrote numerous accomplished film scores in a style reminiscent of Honegger and his contemporaries.

At a glance: Jacques Ibert

Born:	1890
Died:	1955
Must listen:	*The Italian Straw Hat* (1928), *Don Quixote* (1934), *Golgotha* (1935), *Macbeth* (1948), *Invitation to the Dance* (1956)

Ibert originally wanted to be an actor and brought his passion for drama into every medium in which he worked. He stepped in to write the music for Georg Pabst's adaptation of *Don Quixote* when health problems prevented Maurice Ravel from completing the score. The film featured the Russian bass Feodor Chaliapin and the soundtrack was more or less a showcase for singer and orchestra. For *Golgotha*, the first full portrayal of Jesus Christ in a sound film, Ibert also made use of the Ondes Martenot. His music for Orson Welles' *Macbeth* is a mixture of eerie sounds emerging from a selection of exotic percussion, as well as brilliant brass writing for the battles.

The British

Arthur Benjamin studied composition at the Royal College of Music in London under Charles Villiers Stanford before pursuing a career as a piano professor, conductor and composer.

At a glance: Arthur Benjamin

Born: 1893
Died: 1960
Must listen: *The Man Who Knew Too Much* (1934), *Turn of the Tide* (1935), *An Ideal Husband* (1947), *Fire Down Below* (1957), *The Naked Earth* (1958)

Benjamin was approached to write his first film score, *The Scarlet Pimpernel* (1934), by one of his pupils Muir Matheson, who had become music director of the London Films Studio. For Hitchcock, Benjamin composed the dramatic "*Storm Cloud Cantata*", which plays an important part in the climax to *The Man Who Knew Too Much*. After a spell in Canada working as a conductor and teacher, Benjamin returned to Britain and produced nine further film scores before his death. Benjamin was among the few early film composers concerned about how the music would actually sound through cinema speakers. He deliberately pared down his orchestration to aim for the clearest possible sound quality.

Among the composers who, for financial reasons, could not say no to the movies, **Sir Arthur Bliss** was among the most distinguished.

At a glance: Arthur Bliss

Born: 1891
Died: 1975
Must listen: *Things to Come* (1936), *Conquest of the Air* (1938), *Men of Two Worlds* (1946), *Christopher Columbus* (1949)

Like Arthur Benjamin, Bliss also came from the era of Elgar and Stanford but enjoyed experimenting on a series of avant-garde concert works, including *Colour Symphony* (1922). *Things to Come*, his landmark movie score, set a new standard for the genre – symphonic in scope and able to hold its own in the concert hall and on record.

Film music revived the career of **Sir Arnold Bax**, one of Britain's most sophisticated composers.

At a glance: Arnold Bax

Born: 1883
Died: 1953
Must listen: *Malta GC* (1942), *Oliver Twist* (1948), *Journey into History* (1948)

A devotee of Wagner, Bax wrote music that absorbed influences from many cultures –

including Irish, Norwegian and Russian. Bax had composed all his most famous music, including the tone poem *Tintagel*, by the time the Second World War began.

Despite being appointed Master of the King's Music, he felt drained of his creative energies. Just as he was contemplating retirement, an offer came to write for the cinema – a medium in which he had little interest and no experience. *Malta GC* was Bax's only contribution to the Crown Film Unit's war effort. His score for *Oliver Twist* is among his masterpieces, despite the fact that Bax loathed Dickens' book. Bax gave prominence to a piano in the score, played by Harriet Cohen, with whom he had a long-running extra-marital affair.

Benjamin Frankel gained recognition at the end of the Second World War with some excellent chamber

At a glance: Benjamin Frankel

Born:	1906
Died:	1953
Must listen:	*Trottie True* (1949), *So Long at the Fair* (1950), *The Importance of Being Earnest* (1952), *A Kid for Two Farthings* (1955), *The Prisoner* (1955), *The Curse of the Werewolf* (1961), *The Night of the Iguana* (1964), *Battle of the Bulge* (1965)

music before becoming reportedly the highest paid British film composer of the 1950s.

Frankel wrote eight symphonies, an opera, music for almost 70 films and television programmes and a violin concerto in memory of the victims of the Holocaust. He was an enthusiast for the "serialist" style of composition pioneered by Schoenberg and based his acclaimed *Curse of the Werewolf* score on its principles.

William Alwyn, professor of composition at the Royal Academy of Music for 30 years, wrote more than 70 film scores.

At a glance: William Alwyn

Born: 1905

Died: 1985

Must listen: *Odd Man Out* (1947), *The Fallen Idol*
(1948), *The History of Mr Polly* (1949), *The Crimson Pirate* (1952)

Alwyn considered himself a late Romantic composer who nevertheless loved to make use of dissonance when the occasion demanded it. He even developed his own version of Schoenberg's 12-tone serialism and used it in his soundtrack to *The Black Tent* (1956). His two most famous scores, *Odd Man Out* and *The Fallen Idol*, were the fruit of an excellent partnership with director Carol Reed. Alwyn liked *Odd Man Out* so much that he reused its theme in his first symphony.

The giant of 20th-century British music, **Ralph Vaughan Williams** was another composer who re-used his film music in the concert hall.

At a glance: Ralph Vaughan Williams

Born: 1872

Died: 1958

Must listen: *The 49th Parallel* (1941), *Coastal Command* (1942), *The Loves of Joanna Godden* (1948), *Scott of the Antarctic* (1948)

Vaughan Williams is up there with Elgar as Classic FM listeners' favourite British composer. *The Lark Ascending* may have topped the *Classic FM Hall of Fame* poll, but his film music is less well known. Vaughan Williams' first venture into film music was for *The 49th Parallel*, starring Laurence Olivier, the story of a stranded U-boat trying to find its way into neutral waters. It showed that the composer was as serious and thoughtful about his film scores as he was about his major works for the concert hall. His music was at its most dramatic when it depicted human beings battling against the elements of nature, as in his opera, *Riders to the Sea* (1925–1932). The extraordinary score for *Scott of the Antarctic* (1948), with its wordless choir blizzard, organ-blasting glaciers and evocations of glittering ice floes, was used five years later as the basis for Vaughan Williams' seventh symphony, *Sinfonia Antarctica*.

Willam Walton first got involved with film music through his association with the director/producer Paul Czinner.

At a glance: William Walton

Born: 1902
Died: 1983
Must listen: *The First of the Few* (1942), *Henry V* (1944),
             Hamlet (1948), *Richard III* (1956)

Walton wrote four soundtracks for Czinner, including his first Shakespeare film, *As You Like It* (1936), which starred Laurence Olivier. After scoring five wartime films including *The First of the Few*, from which his popular *Spitfire Prelude and Fugue* was taken, Walton was approached by Olivier to write the music for *Henry V*. The composer was nominated for an Oscar® for his brilliantly colourful score, filled with brassy heroic battle scenes, Renaissance pastiches and pastoral romanticism.

Walton provided Olivier with further scores for *Hamlet*, *Richard III* and *Three Sisters* (1970). His thrilling music for *The Battle of Britain* (1969) was dropped in favour of a score by Ron Goodwin. Olivier, who was appearing in the film, threatened to remove his name from the credits unless Walton's music was used. As a result, some of Walton's score – for the battle sequence – was reinstated.

There were few British composers in the 20th century who were more versatile than **Sir Malcolm Arnold**.

At a glance: Malcolm Arnold

Born: 1921

Died: 2006

Must listen: *The Sound Barrier* (1952), *Hobson's Choice* (1954), *Bridge on the River Kwai* (1957), *The Inn of the Sixth Happiness* (1958), *Whistle Down the Wind* (1961)

Arnold started life as a trumpeter before opting to compose full time. Not only did he write nine symphonies, five ballets, two operas, some 20 concertos and countless other orchestral and chamber works, he composed the music for scores of films, including the award-winning *Bridge on the River Kwai* and *Inn of the Sixth Happiness*.

Arnold loved working on soundtracks, describing it as "immensely liberating". For *Kwai*, the producers wanted the film released in time to be considered for the Oscars®. However, they had been unable to secure a composer willing to write all of the music in under two weeks. Arnold, with whom director David Lean had worked twice before, accepted the challenge. The speed at which he composed and his natural gift for orchestration and melody made him an ideal collaborator for directors.

Sir Richard Rodney Bennett is another British composer who has excelled across musical genres.

At a glance: Richard Rodney Bennett

Born: 1936

Must listen: *Far from the Madding Crowd* (1967), *Nicholas and Alexandra* (1971), *Murder on the Orient Express* (1974), *The Return of the Soldier* (1982), *Four Weddings and a Funeral* (1994)

Rigorously trained in the modernist style under Pierre Boulez, Bennett has composed more than 200 works for the concert hall and some 50 scores for films. He is also an enthusiastic collector and performer of jazz songs. Bennett received Oscar® nominations for *Far from the Madding Crowd*, *Nicholas and Alexander* and *Murder on the Orient Express*, which boasts a marvellous waltzing theme that takes off and powers along like the eponymous steam train.

Following in the footsteps of Sir Arnold Bax and Sir Arthur Bliss, **Malcolm Williamson** was a Master of

At a glance: Malcolm Williamson

Born: 1931

Died: 2003

Must listen: *The Brides of Dracula* (1960), *The Horror of Frankenstein* (1970), *Crescendo* (1972)

the Queen's Music who created music for the cinema.

An Australian by birth and Roman Catholic by conversion, Williamson was immersed in the music of French composer Olivier Messiaen. The majority of his film work was for the Hammer Studios. For the thriller *Crescendo*, Williamson's music plays a key role in the story of a woman writing her thesis about a dead composer.

The director Peter Greenaway and British composer **Michael Nyman** enjoyed a partnership that resulted in Nyman breaking into the mainstream.

At a glance: Michael Nyman

Born: 1944

Must listen: *The Draughtsman's Contract* (1982), *A Zed and Two Noughts* (1985), *Prospero's Books* (1991), *The Piano* (1993), *Gattaca* (1997), *The End of the Affair* (1999), *The Claim* (2000), *The Libertine* (2004)

As an academic writer on music, it was Nyman who first coined the term "minimalism" in relation to the style of music built on subtly shifting, repetitive patterns. The genre served him well in his squawking, highly rhythmic scores for Greenaway. In 1993, his sensuous, folk-inspired music for Jane Campion's *The Piano* was a huge commercial success, selling more than three million copies worldwide.

The Americans

George Antheil was an American composer and pianist who enjoyed friendships in Paris with Stravinsky, James Joyce and Ernest Hemingway before composing some 30 scores.

At a glance: George Antheil

Born: 1900
Died: 1959
Must listen: *In a Lonely Place* (1950), *Dementia* (1955),
            The Pride and the Passion (1957)

One of the more colourful characters in American classical music, Antheil frequently injured himself with his vigorous piano playing. *Ballet Mécanique* (1924) is his best known work and it was turned into an experimental film by the artist Fernand Léger in 1924. *Dementia*, a horror film with no dialogue at all, is considered his finest score. Antheil also patented a torpedo guidance system and a cryptography technique with the actress Hedy Lamarr – and offered relationship advice in newspaper columns!

Aaron Copland developed a distinctive, bucolic sound that evoked the country's wide-open spaces and lent itself well to movies about small-town America.

Copland's first major movie success was the music to an adaptation of John Steinbeck's *Of Mice and*

At a glance: Aaron Copland

Born: 1900
Died: 1980
Must listen: *The City* (1939), *Of Mice and Men* (1939),
            Our Town (1940), *North Star* (1943), *The
            Red Pony* (1949), *The Heiress* (1949)

Men – a formula that was repeated with *The Red Pony.*

Scoring just eight movies, Copland won an Oscar® for his music for *The Heiress*, starring Montgomery Clift. There are few film composers – particularly for westerns – who haven't been influenced by Copland's movie scores or cowboy ballets.

One of the most influential and talented of American musicians, **Leonard Bernstein** wrote just one film score but left his mark on the whole 20th century.

At a glance: Leonard Bernstein

Born: 1918
Died: 1990
Must listen: *On the Town* (1949), *On the Waterfront*
            (1954), *West Side Story* (1961)

Leonard Bernstein was a polymath – a pianist, conductor, educator, showman, writer of musicals,

symphonies and operas. His only film score, *On the Waterfront*, is at once tense, dramatic and lyrical, featuring all the trademark rhythms and harmonies that would become so familiar in Bernstein's masterpiece, the musical *West Side Story*.

The most popular of today's American classical composers, **Philip Glass** has combined his film work with numerous operas, concert works and popular albums.

At a glance: Philip Glass

Born: 1937

Must listen: *Koyaanisqatsi* (1983), *Mishima: A Life in Four Chapters* (1985), *Candyman* (1992), *Kundun* (1997), *The Truman Show* (1998), *The Hours* (2002), *Notes on a Scandal* (2006)

Glass studied mathematics and philosophy before attending Juilliard and learning composition with Darius Milhaud and Nadia Boulanger. His discovery of Indian and African music had a profound effect on his own works. *Koyaanisqatsi* is a unique piece of cinema, perfectly combining music and images. Glass's hypnotic and repetitive works are considered indistinguishable from one another by some, but, nevertheless, they have created a powerful atmosphere for many films.

Cinematic lives of the great composers

The lives of the great classical composers have often provided fascinating subject matter for movies, although, on most occasions, there has been little resemblance between the facts of a composer's life and his story on screen. Starting in the 1940s, "biopics" of great composers, in which classical music was fully integrated into the films' soundtracks, became extremely popular. At the same time, other dramas centred around a leading character who was a great musician, for example *Humoresque* (1946), starring Joan Crawford.

The outrageous British director **Ken Russell** (1927–) has done much to bring the music of the great composers to filmgoers' attention, while playing fast and loose with the facts and adding fantasy elements that are distinctly Russell's own. After producing exquisite documentaries for BBC television on, among others, Elgar, Bartok, Delius, Debussy and Richard Strauss, Russell turned his attention to vivid adaptations of D.H. Lawrence novels and controversial composer biopics, covering the lives of Mahler, Tchaikovsky and Liszt. A fan of great soundtracks himself, Ken Russell presented a series on film music, *Ken Russell's Movie Classics*, on Classic FM in the mid–1990s.

Here is a list of some great composers who have been portrayed on screen and the actors who played them in some of the more interesting cinematic versions of their lives:

Ludwig van Beethoven – played by Gary Oldman in *Immortal Beloved* (1995) and Ed Harris in *Copying Beethoven* (2006)

Hector Berlioz – played by Jean-Louis Barrault in *La symphonie fantastique* (1940)

Frédéric Chopin – played by Cornel Wilde in *A Song to Remember* (1944) and Hugh Grant in *Impromptu* (1989)

George Gershwin – played by Robert Alda in *Rhapsody in Blue* (1945)

Gilbert and Sullivan – played by Nigel Bruce and Claud Allister in *Lillian Russell* (1941), Robert Morley and Maurice Evans in *The Story of Gilbert and Sullivan* (1953) and Jim Broadbent and Allan Corduner in *Topsy Turvy* (1999).

Edvard Grieg – played by Toralv Maurstad in *Song of Norway* (1970)

Georg Frideric Handel –played by Wilfred Lawson in *The Great Mr. Handel* (1942)

Franz Liszt – played by Dirk Bogarde in *Song Without End* (1960) and Roger Daltrey in *Lisztomania* (1975)

Gustav Mahler – played by Robert Powell in *Mahler* (1974)

Wolfgang Amadeus Mozart – played by Tom Hulce in *Amadeus* (1984)

Niccolò Paganini – played by Stewart Granger in
The Magic Bow (1947)

Robert Schumann – played by Paul Henreid in
Song of Love (1947)

Dmitry Shostakovich – played by Ben Kingsley in
Testimony (1988)

Johann Strauss II – played by Kerwin Matthews in
The Waltz King (1960) and Horst Buchholz in
The Great Waltz (1972)

Pyotr Ilyich Tchaikovsky – played by Frank
Sundstrom in *Song of my Heart* (1947) and
Richard Chamberlain in *The Music Lovers* (1970)

Richard Wagner – played by Alan Badel in *Magic
Fire* (1956), Trevor Howard in *Ludwig* (1973),
Paul Nicholas in *Lisztomania* (1976) and Richard
Burton in *Wagner* (1983)

More composers are portrayed in the Italian film
Casa Ricordi (1954) than in any other movie. The
film tells the story of the legendary music
publishing family, the Ricordis. The soundtrack
featured the voices of some of the great opera
singers of the day, including Tito Gobbi, Renata
Tebaldi and Mario del Monaco. Playing the great
composers were Maurice Ronet as Bellini, Marcello
Mastroianni as Donizetti, Gabriele Ferzetti as
Puccini, Roland Alexandre as Rossini and Fosco
Giachetti as Verdi.

Classical stars in movies

Many great classical music stars have popped up in films over the decades. In the golden age of Hollywood, classical acts were often brought in to play their party pieces, to add a touch of class to a revue format. Here are a few classical artists who made an impact on the movies:

The glamorous American soprano **Grace Moore** (1898–1947) became a major Hollywood star in the 1930s. *One Night of Love* (1934) was a huge success, winning her an Oscar® nomination. She died in a plane crash in Denmark in 1947 and Hollywood promptly made a biopic about her called *So This is Love* (1953).

In his first film, *That Midnight Kiss* (1949), tenor **Mario Lanza** (1921–1959) played an unlikely truck driver who becomes an opera singer. Lanza's finest moment was *The Great Caruso* (1951) in which he played his role model, the legendary tenor Enrico Caruso. Despite a career cut short by alcohol, drugs and other problems, Lanza has become a singing legend, selling millions of records all over the world.

Austrian tenor **Richard Tauber** (1892–1948) played Franz Schubert in *Blossom Time* (1934). The following year, in *Heart's Desire*, he played a Viennese beer garden singer brought to London to play a gondolier in an opera.

Tonight We Sing (1953) was a biopic of the
American impresario Sol Hurok and featured
many classical stars of the era, including the
Italian bass **Ezio Pinza** (1892–1957) and the
violinist **Isaac Stern** (1920–2001).

In the Deanna Durbin vehicle *One Hundred Men
and a Girl* (1937), Durbin manages to persuade
the conductor **Leopold Stokowski** (1882–1977)
to direct her ragbag orchestra of musicians and
get them a radio contract. Stokowski appeared
on screen again as himself, conducting the
musical sequences in Disney's *Fantasia* (1940)
and later popped up in *Carnegie Hall* (1947),
along with fellow conductors Walter Damrosch,
Bruno Walter, Artur Rodzinski and Fritz
Reiner; singers Rise Stevens, Lily Pons, Jan
Peerce and Ezio Pinza; pianist Arthur
Rubinstein; cellist Gregor Piatigorsky and
violinist Jascha Heifetz.

The famous Wagnerian tenor **Lauritz Melchior**
(1890–1973) made his movie debut opposite
swimming star Esther Williams in a mountain
lodge love story. He appeared again in *Luxury
Liner* (1948), a musical set on board a ship.

American mezzo-soprano **Gladys Swarthout** (1904–
1969) made five movies for Paramount in the
1930s. In *Rose of the Rancho* (1935), she played a
Zorro-like figure who leads the ranchers against a
bunch of villains.

Luciano Pavarotti (1935–2007) was not quite so
successful at breaking into movies as were his

operatic predecessors. His only film, *Yes, Giorgio* (1982), was an old-fashioned romantic movie that flopped dismally at the box office.

Carmen on screen

Bizet's opera *Carmen* has always fascinated filmmakers, inspiring more than 70 films including some 40 silent movie versions. Cecil B. DeMille cast Metropolitan Opera star Geraldine Farrar in the 1915 version, although not a single note was heard from her. Carmen has been played by such luminaries as Theda Bara in *Carmen* (1915), Dolores del Rio in *The Loves of Carmen* (1927), Rita Hayworth in *The Loves of Carmen* (1948) and Beyoncé Knowles in *Carmen: A Hip Hopera* (2001). In Charlie Chaplin's *Burlesque on Carmen* (1916), Don José is reinvented as "Darn Hosiery". In the all-black *Carmen Jones* (1954), Dorothy Dandridge's singing part was dubbed by a 19-year old music student called Marilyn Horne who was paid $300 for her role. Horne went on to become one of the greatest opera stars of the post-war period. A 1983 flamenco version by Carlos Saura was a big success, while *U-Carmen e-Khayelitsha* (2005) set the opera in a modern-day South African township. In *Babe* (1995), the story of a pig that wants to be a sheepdog, a trio of mice sing the "*Toreador Song*".

20 classical pieces featured in films

The popularity of certain great classical works has been completely revitalized by their use in a movie. Ten such pieces can be found on the CD with this *Friendly Guide*. Here is a list of them plus 10 more that have become favourites after their inclusion in box office hits.

1	*2001: A Space Odyssey*	Richard Strauss: *Also Sprach Zarathustra*, "*Sunrise*"
2	*Apocalypse Now*	Wagner: *Ride of the Valkyries*
3	*Babe*	Saint-Saëns: Organ Symphony, 4th movement
4	*Brief Encounter*	Rachmaninov: Piano Concerto No. 2
5	*Chariots of Fire*	Allegri: Miserere
6	*A Clockwork Orange*	Beethoven: Symphony No. 9, "*Ode to Joy*"
7	*Death in Venice*	Mahler: Symphony No. 5, 4th movement, Adagietto
8	*Diva*	Catalani: *La Wally*, "*Ebben? Ne andrò lontana*"
9	*Driving Miss Daisy*	Dvořák: *Rusalka*, "*Song to the Moon*"
10	*Elvira Madigan*	Mozart: Piano Concerto No. 21, 2nd movement
11	*Excalibur*	Orff: *Carmina Burana*, "*O Fortuna*"
12	*Fantasia*	Dukas: *The Sorcerer's Apprentice*

That's All, Folks!

Whether it's a hippo in a tutu pirouetting to
Ponchielli's' *"Dance of the Hours"* in *Fantasia*, Elmer
Fudd chasing Bugs Bunny across mountaintops
rasping "Kill da Wabbit" in *What's Opera, Doc?* or
Randy Newman singing *"You've Got a Friend in Me"*
over the opening credits of *Toy Story*, there's no
doubt that music and animation have been happy
bedfellows since the earliest days of cinema.

As far back as 1919, the Fleischer brothers – whose
studio went on to put Betty Boop and Popeye on
screen – had worked with a basic process for adding
sound to film. They also invented the bouncing ball
over lyrics to "sing-along" films to help audiences
keep in time with the music pumping out of the

cinema's organ. The Fleischers' *My Old Kentucky Home* in 1926 was probably the first sound cartoon. Max Fleischer didn't believe sound would catch on and held back, allowing Walt Disney to steal the brothers' thunder.

Everything changed with the release of *The Jazz Singer* (1927) and the arrival of the "talkies". Animation studios were among the first to explore the possibilities of sound. For *Steamboat Willie* (1928), his third short starring Mickey Mouse, Walt Disney added an original score and sound effects. The cartoon got a better reception than the main feature.

At a glance: Carl Stalling

Born:	1891
Died:	1972
Must listen:	*The Skeleton Dance* (1929), *A Corny Concerto* (1943), *The Rabbit of Seville* (1950)

Carl Stalling has been called the 20th-century's most famous unknown composer. He wrote the soundtracks for literally hundreds of animated shorts. Anyone who has ever watched a *Looney Tunes* cartoon will have heard his clever, frenetic music. Stalling was working as an organist in Kansas City when he was recruited by Walt Disney to be his musical director. As sound took off, Stalling suggested that Disney launch a series of shorts that would tell their stories through music. The *Silly Symphonies* series began with *Skeleton Dance* (1929).

Stalling left Disney in 1930 and later joined Warner Brothers where he averaged one score a week for more than 2 decades. He was the master of the musical joke, shamelessly referencing and playing with popular song tunes and classical pieces.

At a glance: Scott Bradley

Born: 1891
Died: 1977
Must listen: *The Night Before Christmas* (1941), *Red Hot Riding Hood* (1943), *The Cat Concerto* (1947)

Scott Bradley scored hundreds of cartoons for MGM, including the best of *Tom and Jerry* and Tex Avery's most anarchic outings. Bradley was another Hollywood composer who had studied under Arnold Schoenberg. He wrote his first cartoon scores for Disney's former chief animator Ub Iwerks. In 1937, Bradley was contracted permanently to MGM, even bringing Schoenberg's revolutionary musical ideas into his cartoon scores, which were considered to be more serious and difficult than Carl Stalling's.

At a glance: Frank Churchill

Born: 1901
Died: 1942
Must listen: *The Three Little Pigs* (1933), *Snow White and the Seven Dwarfs* (1937), *Dumbo* (1941), *Bambi* (1942)

Frank Churchill was a medical school dropout who played the piano in cinemas and on the radio. He joined the Disney studios in 1930 and had a huge hit with "Who's Afraid of the Big Bad Wolf?" from *The Three Little Pigs*. His songs for *Snow White* became worldwide favourites. Sadly, Churchill committed suicide at the age of 40. He received two posthumous Oscar® nominations – for his work on *Bambi*.

At a glance: Oliver Wallace

Born: 1887

Died: 1963

Must listen: *Dumbo* (1941), *Der Fuehrer's Face* (1942), *Toot, Whistle, Plunk and Boom* (1953), *Peter Pan* (1953)

London-born **Oliver Wallace** was another composer who started out playing the organ in cinemas. He joined Disney in 1936 and wrote the music for more than 100 shorts. He won his only Oscar® for *Dumbo*, before going on to score *Cinderella, Alice in Wonderland, Peter Pan* and *Lady and the Tramp*. Wallace was a master at incorporating the song tunes from the films into the background music.

At a glance: George Bruns

Born: 1914

Died: 1983

Must listen: *Sleeping Beauty* (1959), *The Sword in the Stone* (1964)

George Bruns began his career writing the music for *Mr Magoo* shorts. A composer from the next generation of Disney films, Bruns received four Oscar® nominations for his work, which also included *101 Dalmatians* (1961) and incidental music for *The Jungle Book* (1967).

At a glance: Richard M. Sherman/Robert B. Sherman

Born: 1925/1928

Must listen: *Mary Poppins* (1964), *The Jungle Book* (1967)

The Sherman Brothers' music had a profound impact on Disney's fortunes in the 1960s. They won two Oscars® for *Mary Poppins* while *The Jungle Book* remains among Disney's best loved scores.

At a glance: Alan Menken

Born: 1949

Must listen: *The Little Mermaid* (1989), *Beauty and the Beast* (1991), *Aladdin* (1992), *Pocahontas* (1994), *The Hunchback of Notre Dame* (1996)

After a fallow period in the 1970s and 1980s, Disney's cartoon feature output was re-animated with a succession of musical spectaculars, penned by **Alan Menken**. After meeting lyricist Howard Ashman at a musical theatre workshop, the pair had a stage and screen hit with *Little Shop of Horrors*.

With Disney's return to lavish features, Menken and Ashman's *The Little Mermaid* became the highest grossing animated film up to that point. *Beauty and the Beast* became the first animated feature to receive a Best Picture nomination at the Oscars®. Ashman wrote several lyrics for *Aladdin* before his untimely death. Menken completed the score with British lyricist Tim Rice. Menken went on to work with Broadway tunesmith Stephen Schwartz on *Pocahontas* and *The Hunchback of Notre Dame*. Menken continued his relationship with Disney on *Hercules* (1997), *Home on the Range* (2004) and, most recently, *Enchanted* (2007).

With the emergence of brilliant young talent all over the world, animation has enjoyed a new lease of life in the past decade as one of cinema's most lucrative genres. The increasing sophistication of computer-generated animation has seen a proliferation of highly entertaining family films – from the likes of Pixar and Dreamworks, as well as Disney – while the British-based Aardman Animations revived "stop-motion" animation to universal adulation with their *Wallace and Gromit* films (1989–2008) and *Chicken Run* (2000). From Hans Zimmer's stable, **Harry Gregson-Williams** (1961–) and **John Powell** (1963–) have emerged with a particular talent for writing music for animated features, producing excellent scores for *Chicken Run* and the *Shrek* films (2001–2007). More recently, **Michael Giacchino** (1967–) has emerged from writing music for video games to scoring some of Pixar's biggest hits, including *The Incredibles* (2004) and *Ratatouille* (2007).

Classics and the cartoons

While you might be thinking that Disney's *Fantasia* (1940) was the first animated film to match hand-drawn images with classical music, it was, in fact, as far back as 1928 that the pioneering silhouette animator Lotte Reiniger was working with such musical giants as Paul Hindemith and Kurt Weill on a feature-length version of *Dr Dolittle*. Another of Reiniger's projects was an animated version of Ravel's *L'enfants et les sortilèges*.

As animation techniques became more sophisticated, cartoonists found classical music to be a good source of inspiration as well as a prime target for their gags. In Mickey Mouse's first colour cartoon, *The Band Concert* (1935), Mickey's best attempts to get his band through a performance of Rossini's overture to *William Tell* are disrupted by Donald Duck noisily selling popcorn and playing "*Turkey in the Straw*" on his flute.

As Donald Duck's popularity overtook that of the mouse, Disney dreamed up the idea of reviving Mickey's career with a starring role in a short based on *The Sorcerer's Apprentice* by Paul Dukas (1865–1935). With the involvement of the Philadelphia

Orchestra's conductor, Leopold Stokowski, the short grew into the much more ambitious *Fantasia* (1940), a full-length animated feature taking the form of a concert of favourite pieces, brought alive with stunning visual sequences by Disney animators. Ever the innovator, Disney even developed an ambitious sound system for *Fantasia* using seven tracks and 30 loudspeakers.

Some of *Fantasia*'s sequences work better than others but the beauty of the animation, its wit and ingenuity, has hardly been bettered. Disney's hope that new segments could be inserted into *Fantasia* from time to time was finally realized with *Fantasia 2000*, a less successful venture but nevertheless featuring some spectacular moments – including a stylized, loosely drawn *Rhapsody in Blue* and a magical interpretation of Stravinsky's *The Firebird*.

In 1943, Warner Brothers took a swipe at *Fantasia* with *A Corny Concerto* in which Bugs Bunny and Porky Pig perform a ballet. A second section sends up Johann Strauss II's *Blue Danube* and Disney's *The Ugly Duckling* (1939), with a baby black duck fighting off a buzzard. The Italian animator Bruno Bozzetto (1933–) also sent up *Fantasia* in *Allegro non Troppo* (1977). Bozzetto's segments, though, are more than a parody. *Allegro*'s six sequences, including those based on Ravel's *Bolero* and Sibelius' *Valse Triste*, are exceptional in their own right.

In the Tom and Jerry short *The Cat Concerto* (1947), Tom tries to perform Liszt's *Hungarian Rhapsody* while Jerry is determined to enjoy his sleep inside the piano. In *Baton Bunny* (1959), Bugs Bunny attempts to conduct an orchestra in *Morning, Noon and Night in Vienna* by Franz von Suppé, while fighting off an annoying fly. In 1960, Chuck Jones made *High Note* in which the sheet music for *The Blue Danube* is constructed on the musical stave by a cast of animated notes and symbols.

What's Opera, Doc?

Of all classical music forms, however, opera has best fed the imagination of Hollywood's greatest animators, with *The Barber of Seville* and the sextet from Donizetti's *Lucia di Lammermoor* popping up most frequently in cartoon classics.

Bugs Bunny's first foray into opera was *Long-Haired Hare* (1949), which features the *Barber* aria "*Largo al factotum*". The following year, *The Rabbit of Seville* (1950) saw Bugs playing the barber to his tormented customer, Elmer Fudd. Woody Woodpecker also tried his hand at opera and hairdressing in *The Barber of Seville* (1944). In *Notes to You* (1941), Porky Pig is kept awake at night by an alley cat howling "*Largo al factotum*". After Porky shoots the cat, a chorus of ghostly felines arrives to sing the *Lucia* sextet. The cartoon was remade in 1948 with Elmer Fudd and Sylvester. Tex

Avery's *The Magical Maestro* (1952) tells the story of a man trying to sing *The Barber of Seville* as a magician persists in transforming his costumes. In Disney's *The Whale who Wanted to Sing at the Met* (1946), Nelson Eddy voiced Willie the whale who can sing tenor, baritone and bass at the same time. Willie dreams of auditioning with "*Largo al factotum*" and the *Lucia* sextet before singing *Pagliacci* at the Met, with the "motley" on, his whale tears requiring the audience to put up umbrellas.

The Disney studio also brought the ultimate diva to cinema screens – Clara Cluck, a full-bodied and not particularly talented chicken, voiced by singer Florence Gill. Clara Cluck sang Juliet to Donald Duck's Romeo in *Mickey's Grand Opera* (1934) and gobbled her way single-handedly through the *Lucia* sextet in *The Orphans' Benefit* (1934).

Animation's finest opera moment by far was *What's Opera, Doc?* (1957) in which Wagner's *Ring* is compressed into just 6 minutes. Elmer Fudd in armour chases Bugs Bunny across mountains, intoning "Kill da wabbit, kill da wabbit" to the tune of the "*Ride of the Valkyries*". Even Pablo Picasso is said to have admired the artistry of *What's Opera, Doc?*

Other cartoon characters encountering opera included Mr Magoo, stumbling his way chaotically

111

through an opera in *Stage Door Magoo* (1955), magpies Heckle and Jeckle in *Off to the Opera* (1952) and Gandy Goose in *Carmen's Veranda* (1944).

What They Say About Film Music . . . and Each Other

On writing film music:

It's not a pleasant experience. I love being asked and I love finishing the job, but the doing of it – I don't know whether I really enjoy it. You have moments of great inspiration and excitement, but I guess it's a bit like climbing Everest.

DAVID ARNOLD

If a film score comes out uninfluenced by Berlioz, it's no good!

MALCOLM ARNOLD

All I need in order to write a film score are the parameters of budget and length. Then, when the film is made, I require a time-coded video to work from. I don't need, or want, to be part of the production team.

RICHARD RODNEY BENNETT

In film music, Bernard Herrmann I'd say would be right at the top of the list; surely David Raksin has done some things which I think are extraordinary, as did Miklós Rózsa, Franz Waxman, certainly; some of Alex North's are absolutely outstanding.

I'll get hold of a film and look at it 20 times. I'll spend one week just looking at the film – once in the morning, once in the afternoon – until the film tells me what to do.

ELMER BERNSTEIN

I almost never try to make the audience comfortable. I wouldn't want that if I were in the audience.

CARTER BURWELL

114

It should sound like good music; it should always have a structure to it. But basically it should be musical and listenable. And it should be able to, away from the picture, conjure up the same sort of feelings and images that it was meant to on screen.

PATRICK DOYLE

For me, writing something in the spirit of Halloween is like Mother Teresa writing on charity and sacrifice. It's just second nature to me.

I don't think there's a trademark Danny Elfman element that has been consistent in my work. I don't hear many similarities in what I do and I don't think it's necessary that I have a particular style. Having a particular style is not bad, but I prefer to push myself in the direction of being a composer who you never know what he's doing next.

DANNY ELFMAN

When Bernard Herrmann in Psycho *took the sound of a screechy bird and sort of morphed it into what it might feel like to be stabbed, the music took on a better, more significant role than a sound effect would have in that scene.*

ELLIOT GOLDENTHAL

Sometimes I say, "Gee, did I write that? It's good!" Sometimes I say, "I'm sorry I wrote that: it's lousy."

If our music survives, which I have no doubt it will, then it will because it is good.

JERRY GOLDSMITH

To Steven Spielberg, who was expressing his admiration for the composer: If ya admire my music so much, why do ya always use Johnny Williams for your pictures?

In California, they like to pigeonhole you. From the time I began working for Hitchcock, they decided I was a big suspense man. On other occasions, I've had fantasies of bittersweet romantic stories. I think I'd enjoy writing a good comedy score, but I've never had the luck to be offered such films. Mancini gets the cheerful ones.

BERNARD HERRMANN

I suddenly realized that I could be as expressive as I wanted. Each film was completely different. To me it was no different than Haydn being kept as a court composer, being paid, having the piece performed and given an orchestra.

JAMES HORNER

I like diversity. It is not good to score too many films of the same type. The problem with Hollywood is that they like to classify you . . . After Lawrence of Arabia *they thought I could only write desert music. Then, after* Zhivago, *that I could only write snow music.*

MAURICE JARRE

Film music is always at the service of another piece of work. It's complementary, but secondary.

I was never influenced by other film composers. I simply developed my own ideas. And I never followed any fashion. I always think that when something is currently very trendy, it's already very old.

On The Mission: *A big theme tune is the thing that an audience can most easily access. The rest of a score is more to do with creating an atmosphere. It's received by the brain, while the big tune touches the brain and the heart.*

ENNIO MORRICONE

The great thing about doing movie music is that you find out what you're capable of. You may think you're incapable of producing a certain rhythm, but it's your job to solve that problem. If you open your mind, an idea will lead you to the next one.

THOMAS NEWMAN

Composers today get a TV script on Friday and have to record on Tuesday. It's just dreadful to impose on gifted talent and expect decent music under these conditions.

I find it practically impossible to score anything which does not move me emotionally and I attempted to convey the internal, rather than external aspects of the film. By this I mean the music was related to the characters at all time and not the action.

ALEX NORTH

When Strauss was writing his music, it was dance music. Now it's classical music. So how can you tell that in 50 years' time film music will not turn out to be classical music?

ZBIGNIEW PREISNER

What you can't do with a camera or dialogue, music has a way of taking care of. It gets at the deeper emotions that aren't always expressible on film. People who are skeptical about the value of film music

*should be condemned to watch films
without it.'*

DAVID RAKSIN

*Film composing is a splendid discipline,
and I recommend a course of it to all
composition teachers whose pupils are apt to
be dawdling in their ideas, or whose every
bar is sacred and must not be cut or
altered.*

RALPH VAUGHAN WILLIAMS

When [Spielberg] showed me Schindler's
List, *I was so moved I could barely speak. I
remember saying to him, "Steven, you need
a better composer than I am to do this
film." And he said, "I know, but they're all
dead."*

*Writing a tune is like sculpting. You get
four or five notes, you take one out and
move one around, and you do a bit more
and eventually, as the sculptor says, "In that
rock there is a statue, we have to go find it."*

*So much of what we do is ephemeral and
quickly forgotten, even by ourselves, so it's
gratifying to have something you have done
linger in people's memories.*

JOHN WILLIAMS

A good score should have a point of view all of its own. It should transcend all that has gone before, stand on its own two feet and still serve the movie. A great soundtrack is all about communicating with the audience, but we all try to bring something extra to the movie that is not entirely evident on screen.

HANS ZIMMER

100 Masters of Movie Music

Here is an easy-to-use, alphabetical overview of the 100 composers whose music you are most likely to hear on *Classic FM at the Movies*. The listing does not include classical composers who have written film music. They are covered in detail in Chapter 8.

Those movie composers we have already mentioned in previous chapters are listed here with a page number, so you can go back and find out more. For the rest, who we were not able to include in the main body of the text, we have given a brief biography, some "Must listen" scores, and noted any Oscar® success.

Richard Addinsell (1904–1977)

British composer working in the theatre and cinema, from the 1930s to the 1960s. His best known work remains the "*Warsaw Concerto*" from *Dangerous Moonlight* (1941).

Must listen: *Gaslight* (1940), *Dangerous Moonlight* (1941), *Blithe Spirit* (1945), *Scrooge* (1951).

John Addison (1920–1998)

British composer who studied at the Royal College of Music. An association with producer–director Roy Boulting led to his working in film from the late 1940s.

Must listen: *Reach for the Sky* (1956), *A Taste of Honey* (1961), *Tom Jones* (1963)

Oscar®-winner: *Tom Jones*

Daniele Amfitheatrof (1901–1983)

Born in Russia, Amfitheatrof studied in Rome. Having worked as a conductor he was contracted to MGM in 1938.

Must listen: *Lassie Come Home* (1943), *Guest Wife* (1945), *Song of the South* (1946). The last two were both nominated for Academy Awards®.

Craig Armstrong (1959–)

Scotsman Armstrong, having studied at London University and the Royal Academy of Music, started composing for the theatre in the late 1980s. Best known for his collaborations with Australian director Baz Luhrmann.

Must listen: *William Shakespeare's Romeo + Juliet*

(1996), *Moulin Rouge* (2001), *The Quiet American* (2002)

David Arnold (1962–)

See page 70

Luis Bacalov (1933–)

Coming from a rock background – Luis Enrique and his Electronic Men – Bacalov has worked in Italian cinema since the 1960s. He found worldwide acclaim with the multi-award winning soundtrack to *Il Postino*.

Must listen: *The Gospel According to St. Matthew* (1965), *Il Postino* (1994)

Oscar® winner: *Il Postino*

Angelo Badalamenti (1937–)

See pages 68–69

Klaus Badelt (1968–)

A successful film and commercial composer in his native Germany, Badelt was invited by Hans Zimmer to work in the USA, where he contributed to *The Thin Red Line* and *The Prince of Egypt*. He also co-produced and co-wrote the massively successful *Gladiator*.

Must listen: *The Prince of Egypt* (1998), *The Thin Red Line* (1998), *Gladiator* (2000), *K–19: The Widowmaker* (2002), *The Time Machine* (2002), *Pirates of the Caribbean: The Curse of the Black Pearl* (2003), *Constantine* (2005)

John Barry (1933–)

See pages 53–54

James Bernard (1925–2001)

See pages 44–45

Elmer Bernstein (1922–2004)

See pages 41–42

Howard Blake (1938–)

Classically trained at the Royal Academy of Music, Blake has been one of Britain's most popular and prolific film composers since the late 1960s. Best known for the song, *"Walking in the Air"* from the TV animation, *The Snowman* (1982).

Must listen: The Duellists (1977), *Victor/Victoria* (1982), *The Hunger* (1983)

Carter Burwell (1955–)

Born in New York and studied at Harvard University, Burwell is best known for his ongoing collaborations with the Coen Brothers.

Must listen: *Blood Simple* (1983), *Barton Fink* (1991), *Fargo*, (1996) *The Big Lebowski* (1998), *The Man who Wasn't There* (2001)

John Carpenter (1948–)

Best known as a horror and science fiction director, Carpenter often scores his own movies.

Must listen: *Dark Star* (1974), *Halloween* (1978), *The Thing* (1982), *Big Trouble in Little China* (1986)

Charles Chaplin (1889–1977)

See pages 22–23

Bill Conti (1942–)

Prolific American composer best known for the *Rocky* and *Karate Kid* series of the 1980s.

Must listen: *Rocky* (1976), *The Right Stuff* (1983), *The Karate Kid* (1984)

Oscar® winner: *The Right Stuff*

Carl Davis (1936–)

See pages 23–24

Don Davis (1957–)

A graduate of UCLA, Davis first worked on TV's *Hart to Hart*. Working mainly in television until the mid-1990s, global success came with his scoring of the *Matrix* trilogy.

Must listen: *Bound* (1996), *The Matrix* (1999)

Georges Delerue (1925–1992)

See pages 46–47

Alexandre Desplat (1961–)

Of mixed French and Greek parentage, Desplat was something of a child prodigy, learning piano, trumpet and flute at a young age. Working in both France and the USA, he has around 100 film credits to his name.

Must listen: *Girl with a Pearl Earring* (2003), *Syriana* (2005), *The Painted Veil* (2006), *The Queen* (2006), *The Golden Compass* (2007), *The Curious Case of Benjamin Button* (2008)

Adolph Deutsch (1897–1980)

British-born arranger, composer and conductor. Worked mainly for MGM and Warner Brothers from the 1930s, throughout the "Golden Age" of cinema.

Must listen: *The Maltese Falcon* (1941), *The Mask of Dimitrios* (1944), *Some Like it Hot* (1959)

Oscar® winners: *Annie Get Your Gun* (1950), *Seven Brides for Seven Brothers* (1954), *Oklahoma* (1955) (all as arranger)

Pino Donaggio (1941–)

Italian composer working both in Italy and Hollywood, best known for his horror soundtracks of the 1980s.

Must listen: *Don't Look Now* (1973), *Dressed to Kill* (1980), *Body Double* (1984)

Patrick Doyle (1953–)

See pages 69–70

Anne Dudley (1956–)

Originally in 1980s "studio boffins" band, The Art of Noise, a series of soundtracks for influential British films eventually led to the global hit *The Full Monty* and mainstream Hollywood success.

Must listen: *Buster* (1988), *The Crying Game* (1992), *The Full Monty* (1997), *American History X* (1998)

Oscar® winner: *The Full Monty*

Brian Easdale (1909–1995)

Educated at the Royal College of Music, Easdale is inextricably linked with the films of Michael Powell and Emeric Pressburger. After their failure *Peeping Tom* (1960), Easdale's career also declined.

Must listen: *Black Narcissus* (1947), *The Red Shoes* (1948), *Peeping Tom* (1960)

Oscar® winner: *The Red Shoes*

Randy Edelman (1947–)

American composer who studied at the University of Cincinnati. After a successful pop career – both as writer and performer – he turned to scoring for TV and eventually movies.

Must listen: *Ghostbusters II* (1989), *The Last of the Mohicans* (1992), *Dragon: The Bruce Lee Story*

(1993), *Dragonheart* (1996), *The Skulls* (2000), *Shanghai Knights* (2003)

Danny Elfman (1949–)

See pages 67–68

George Fenton (1950–)

British composer with a background in television. All the films listed were nominated for Academy Awards®.

Must listen: *Gandhi* (1982), *Cry Freedom* (1987), *Dangerous Liaisons* (1988), *The Fisher King* (1991)

Hugo Friedhofer (1902–1981)

See page 32

Peter Gabriel (1950–)

British composer and singer, he was a co-founder of 1970s' rock giants, Genesis, and an early exponent of "world music".

Must listen: *Birdy* (1984), *The Last Temptation of Christ* (1988), *Rabbit-Proof Fence* (2002)

Michael Giacchino (1967–)

American composer as well known for his work on video games – the *Medal of Honor* and *Call of Duty* series – as well film soundtracks.

Must listen: *The Incredibles* (2004), *Ratatouille* (2007), *Star Trek* (2009)

Elliot Goldenthal (1954–)

See pages 73–74

Jerry Goldsmith (1929–2004)

See page 52

Howard Goodall (1958–)

After studying at Christ Church, Oxford, Goodall has excelled as a composer for choirs, as well as television, stage and films. His film work has been almost entirely for Rowan Atkinson. He has been Classic FM's composer-in-residence and a weekend show presenter since June 2008.

Must listen: *Bean* (1997), *Johnny English* (2003), *Mr Bean's Holiday* (2007)

Ron Goodwin (1925–2003)

Born in Devon, Goodwin studied at the Guildhall School of Music. For 40 years his themes, often for war films, were some of the most instantly recognizable in British cinema.

Must listen: *633 Squadron* (1964), *Those Magnificent Men in their Flying Machines* (1965), *Where Eagles Dare* (1968)

Harry Gregson-Williams (1958–)

Brother of fellow composer Rupert, Gregson-Williams was a chorister at Cambridge and studied at the Guildhall School of Music. He has worked collaboratively with both Stanley Myers and Hans Zimmer.

Must listen: *The Borrowers* (1997), *Chicken Run* (2000), *Shrek* (2001)

Bernard Herrmann (1911–1975)

See pages 34–35

David Hirschfelder (1960–)

With a background in jazz – 1980s' band Pyramid – the Australian composer has worked in movies since the 1990s, collecting an Academy Award® nomination for *Elizabeth* (1998).

Must listen: *Strictly Ballroom* (1992), *Shine* (1996), *Elizabeth* (1998) *Australia* (2008)

James Horner (1953–)

See page 60–61

James Newton Howard (1951–)

See pages 72–73

Maurice Jarre (1924–2009)

See pages 48–49

Karl Jenkins (1944–)

Born and educated in Wales, Jenkins first tasted success with 1970s jazz-rock improvisers, Soft Machine. A prolific career in writing for television has been eclipsed by his multi-million selling classical works, such as *Adiemus: Songs of Sanctuary* and *The Armed Man*, both Classic FM favourites.

Must listen: *Shadows* (1982), *River Queen* (2005)

Jan A. P. Kaczmarek (1953–)

Polish by birth, Kaczmarek lives and works in the USA. After a successful career writing for the stage, he broke through into film, scoring more than 30 features and documentaries.

Must listen: *Pale Blood* (1990), *Washington Square* (1997), *Unfaithful* (2002), *Finding Neverland* (2003)

Oscar® winner: *Finding Neverland*

Michael Kamen (1948–)

See page 62

Bronislau Kaper (1902–1983)

One of the most influential of 20th-century film music composers, Kaper was born and educated in Poland before moving to the USA and being contracted to MGM.

Must listen: *The Chocolate Soldier* (1941), *Invitation* (1952), *The Barretts of Wimpole Street* (1957), *Mutiny on the Bounty* (1962), *Tobruk* (1967)

Oscar® winner: *Lili* (1953)

Wojciech Kilar (1932–)

Composer of Polish background who splits his work between the USA and Europe.

Must listen: *Bram Stoker's Dracula* (1992), *The Portrait of a Lady* (1996), *The Pianist* (2002)

Erich Wolfgang Korngold (1897–1957)

See pages 28–29

Francis Lai (1932–)

See pages 47–48

Michel Legrand (1931–)

See page 48

Henry Mancini (1924–1994)

See page 53

Dario Marianelli (1963–)

See pages 75–76

Jerome Moross (1913–1983)

See pages 42–43

Ennio Morricone (1928–)

See pages 50–51

Stanley Myers (1930–1993)

British theatrical composer who wrote for the movies from the 1960s. His most famous work remains "*Cavatina*", popularized by its use in *The Deer Hunter* (1978).

Must listen: *The Deer Hunter* (1978), *My Beautiful Laundrette* (1985), *Wish You Were Here* (1987)

Mario Nascimbene (1913–2002)

Born and working in Italy, his international success of *The Barefoot Contessa* (1954), swiftly brought Hollywood and British soundtrack work.

Must listen: *The Barefoot Contessa* (1954), *The Vikings* (1958), *One Million Years BC* (1966)

Alfred Newman (1901–1970)

See pages 29–31

David Newman (1954–)

Son of Alfred Newman, David trained at the University of Southern California, specializing in conducting until he turned to film scores in the 1980s.

Must listen: *Heathers* (1989), *The Flintstones* (1994), *Anastasia* (1997), *Galaxy Quest* (1999), *Ice Age* (2002), *The Spirit* (2008)

Randy Newman (1943–)

Established and successful from the 1970s, the American singer–songwriter has picked up many accolades, recently through his work on Pixar productions.

Must listen: *Ragtime* (1981), *Awakenings* (1990), *Toy Story* (1995), *A Bug's Life* (1998), *Pleasantville* (1998), *Monsters, Inc.* (2001), *Seabiscuit* (2003), *Cars* (2006)

Thomas Newman (1955–)

See pages 71–72

Jack Nitzsche (1937–2000)

As renowned in rock music for work with Phil Spector and the Rolling Stones, Nitzsche's parallel

film career took in some of Hollywood's largest
1970s' and 80s' hits.

Must listen: *One Flew over the Cuckoo's Nest*
(1975), *An Officer and a Gentleman* (1982),
Starman (1984), *Jewel of the Nile* (1985)

Oscar® winner: For the song, "*Up Where
We Belong*" from *An Officer and a
Gentleman*

Alex North (1910–1991)

See pages 40–41

John Ottman (1964–)

Born in San Diego and studying at USC film
school, Ottman often works in the horror and
sci-fi genres.

Must listen: *The Usual Suspects* (1995), *Halloween
H2O* (1998), *Lake Placid* (1999), *X–2* (2003),
Superman Returns (2006)

Jean-Claude Petit (1943–)

French composer often working on historical or
period adventures.

Must listen: *Jean de Florette* (1987), *Manon
des Sources* (1987), *Cyrano de Bergerac*
(1990).

Barrington Pheloung (1954–)

Australian composer now living and
working in England, Pheloung is best
known for television work – including
Inspector Morse – and for independent British
films.

Must listen: *Truly Madly Deeply* (1990), *Shopping*
(1993), *Hilary and Jackie* (1998)

Basil Poledouris (1945–2006)

American composer, prolific in films since the 1970s. His scores take in some of Hollywood's biggest adventures and thrillers.

Must listen: *Conan the Barbarian* (1982), *Robocop* (1987), *The Hunt for Red October* (1990), *Starship Troopers* (1997), *Les Misérables* (1998)

Rachel Portman (1960–)

Married to producer Uberto Pasolini, Portman studied at Oxford and since the 1980s has composed scores primarily for period dramas and romances.

Must listen: *Life is Sweet* (1990), *Emma* (1996), *Chocolat* (2000), *Nicholas Nickleby* (2002), *Oliver Twist* (2005), *The Duchess* (2008)

Oscar® winner: *Emma*

John Powell (1963–)

Having studied at Trinity College of Music, the English composer moved to Hollywood where he joined Hans Zimmer's Media Ventures.

Must listen: *Face/Off* (1997), *Chicken Run* (with Harry Gregson-Williams) (2000), *Shrek* (with Harry Gregson-Williams) (2001), *The Bourne Identity* (2002), *Kung Fu Panda* (2008)

Zbigniew Preisner (1955–)

Polish composer who studied in Krakow. Usually associated with the films of Krysztof Kieslowski and Agnieszka Holland.

Must listen: *Europa, Europa* (1990), *The Double Life of Veronique* (1991), *At Play in the Fields of the Lord* (1991), *The Three Colours* trilogy (1994)

Trevor Rabin (1954–)

South African musician and composer now working in Hollywood, via the 80s'/90s' incarnation of rock group, Yes. Best known for adventure films and thrillers.

Must listen: *Con Air* (1997), *Enemy of the State* (1998), *Gone In 60 Seconds* (2000), *National Treasure* (2004)

David Raksin (1912–2004)

See pages 35–36

Alan Rawsthorne (1905–1971)

British composer whose best work came in the immediate post-war years, often with war-related themes.

Must listen: *Burma Victory* (1945), *Saraband for Dead Lovers* (1948), *Where No Vultures Fly* (1951), *The Cruel Sea* (1953), *West of Zanzibar* (1954)

Richard Robbins (1940–)

American composer with association with Merchant Ivory films dating back to the 1970s.

Must listen: *A Room with a View* (1985), *Howard's End* (1992), *The Remains of the Day* (1993)

Leonard Rosenman (1924–)

See pages 43–44

Nino Rota (1911–1979)

See pages 49–50

Miklós Rózsa (1901–1995)

See pages 33–34

Ryuichi Sakamoto (1952–)

See page 60

Hans Salter (1896–1994)

Austrian-born composer who worked in Berlin. Like many, he moved to the USA in the 1930s, where he worked, almost exclusively, for Universal.

Must listen: *The Amazing Mrs Holliday* (1943), *Christmas Holiday* (1944), *This Love of Ours* (1945)

Gustavo Santaolalla (1951–)

See page 75

Philippe Sarde (1945–)

Prolific French composer with only a few English-language films to his name.

Must listen: *Tess* (1979), *Quest for Fire* (1981), *Lord of the Flies* (1990)

Lalo Schifrin (1932–)

Prolific Argentinean composer with a background in jazz, both leading his own band and working with Dizzy Gillespie.

Must listen: *Cool Hand Luke* (1967), *Voyage of the Damned* (1976), *The Amityville Horror* (1979), *The Sting 2* (1983)

Ilona Sekacz (1948–)

Of mixed Polish/English parentage, Sekacz was a member of the National Youth Orchestra and wrote for both the Royal Shakespeare Company and the National Theatre. Since the 1990s she has composed for "little seen, art-house" films.

Must listen: *A Pin for the Butterfly* (1994), *Antonia's Line* (1995), *Mrs Dalloway* (1997), *Wondrous Oblivion* (2003)

Eric Serra (1959–)

French composer best known for his work with director/producer Luc Besson.

Must listen: *La femme Nikita* (1990), *Leon* (1994), *The Fifth Element* (1997).

Marc Shaiman (1959–)

American composer and arranger who contributed to some of the biggest Hollywood hits of the 1990s.

Must listen: *Misery* (1990), *City Slickers* (1991), *The American President* (1995), *The Bucket List* (2007)

Oscar® winner: *The First Wives Club* (1996)

Howard Shore (1946–)

See pages 66–67

Alan Silvestri (1950)

Prolific New York-born composer. His soundtrack work runs the gamut from comedy to horror, via adventure and drama. He has enjoyed a longstanding collaboration with director Robert Zemeckis.

Must listen: *Back to the Future* (1985), *Who Framed Roger Rabbit* (1988), *Forrest Gump* (1994), *The Mummy Returns* (2001), *Beowulf* (2007)

Max Steiner (1888–1971)

See pages 26–28

Toru Takemitsu (1930–1996)

Japanese composer who worked predominantly in his native land with directors such as Kurosawa, although he did make occasional Hollywood hits

Must listen: *Empire of Passion* (1980), *Ran* (1985), *Black Rain* (1989)

Tan Dun (1957–)

A highly successful Chinese contemporary classical composer, Tan Dun's best known in the west for martial arts epics.

Must listen: *Crouching Tiger, Hidden Dragon* (2000), *Hero* (2002)

Oscar® winner: *Crouching Tiger, Hidden Dragon*

Mikis Theodorakis (1925–)

See page 51

Yann Tiersen (1970–)

French composer best known for the score to *Amélie* (2001). Primarily writing for the piano, he also works with more obscure, and even "toy" instruments. Elements of "minimalism" means he naturally draws comparisons with Philip Glass and Michael Nyman.

Must listen: *Amélie* (*Le fabuleux destin d'Amélie Poulain*) (2001), *Goodbye Lenin!* (2003)

Oscar® winner: *Amélie*

Dimitri Tiomkin (1894–1979)

See pages 38–39

Vangelis (1943–)

See page 59

Stephen Warbeck (1953–)

Beginning his career as an actor, Warbeck switched to scoring for television and film.

Must listen: *Shakespeare in Love* (1998), *Billy*

Elliott (2000), *Captain Corelli's Mandolin* (2001), *Charlotte Gray* (2001), *Proof* (2005)
Oscar® winner: *Shakespeare in Love*

Franz Waxman (1906–1967)

See page 33

Roy Webb (1888–1982)

American composer whose life and work encompassed the entire 20th century, while perhaps not achieving the greatness of some of his contemporaries.

Must listen: *Cat People* (1942), *Notorious* (1946), *Mighty Joe Young* (1949)

John Williams (1932–)

See pages 57–59

Debbie Wiseman (1963–)

A graduate of the Guildhall School of Music and Drama, initial scoring for television has now been superseded by film work.

Must listen: *Wilde* (1997), *The Guilty* (2000), *Lighthouse* (2000), *Tom's Midnight Garden* (2000), *Arsène Lupin* (2004)

Gabriel Yared (1949–)

See pages 62, 74

Victor Young (1900–1956)

See pages 31–32

Hans Zimmer (1958–)

See pages 63–66

And the Winner is . . .

The Academy Awards® – or Oscars® – presented each year in Los Angeles by the Academy of Motion Picture Arts and Sciences are the most prestigious, coveted and eagerly anticipated of all movie awards. The first Oscars® ceremony was held in 1929, although the award for musical scoring was not established until 1934. At various points in the Oscars'® history, there have been two awards for music – at times one for scoring and one for adaptation (of a stage musical, for example). In other years, Oscars® have been given for dramatic score and for musical or comedy score. For the purposes of this table, we have limited the listing to those awards given for music especially composed for films, rather than adaptations of stage shows or songs.

The British Academy of Film and Television Awards, or BAFTAs, have risen in prestige over the years and are now considered to be the British equivalent of the Oscars®. They began in 1948 but presentation of an award for film music only commenced in 1968.

Year	OSCAR®	BAFTA
1934	Victor Schertziner and Gus Kahn *One Night of Love*	
1935	Max Steiner *The Informer*	
1936	Erich Wolfgang Korngold *Anthony Adverse*	
1937	Charles Previn *100 Men and a Girl*	
1938	Erich Wolfgang Korngold *The Adventures of Robin Hood*	
1939	Richard Hageman, et al. *Stagecoach*	
1940	Alfred Newman *Tin Pan Alley*	
1941	Bernard Hermann *All that Money Can Buy*	
1942	Max Steiner *Now, Voyager*	
1943	Alfred Newman *The Song of Bernadette*	
1944	Max Steiner *Since You Went Away*	
1945	Miklós Rózsa *Spellbound*	

Year	OSCAR®	BAFTA
1946	Hugo Friedhofer *The Best Years of Our Lives*	
1947	Miklós Rózsa *A Double Life*	
1948	Brian Easdale *The Red Shoes*	
1949	Aaron Copland *The Heiress*	
1950	Franz Waxman *Sunset Boulevard*	
1951	Franz Waxman *A Place in the Sun*	
1952	Dimitri Tiomkin *High Noon*	
1953	Bronislau Kaper *Lili*	
1954	Dimitri Tiomkin *The High and the Mighty*	
1955	Alfred Newman *Love Is a Many-Splendored Thing*	
1956	Victor Young *Around the World in Eighty Days*	
1957	Malcolm Arnold *The Bridge on the River Kwai*	
1958	Dmitri Tiomkin *The Old Man and the Sea*	
1959	Miklós Rósza *Ben-Hur*	
1960	Ernest Gold *Exodus*	
1961	Henry Mancini *Breakfast at Tiffany's*	
1962	Maurice Jarre *Lawrence of Arabia*	
1963	John Addison *Tom Jones*	

Year	OSCAR®	BAFTA
1964	Richard M. and Robert B. Sherman *Mary Poppins*	
1965	Maurice Jarre *Dr Zhivago*	
1966	John Barry *Born Free*	
1967	Elmer Bernstein *Thoroughly Modern Millie*	
1968	John Barry *The Lion in Winter*	John Barry *The Lion in Winter*
1969	Burt Bacharach *Butch Cassidy and the Sundance Kid*	Mikis Theodorakis *Z*
1970	Francis Lai *Love Story*	Burt Bacharach *Butch Cassidy and the Sundance Kid*
1971	Michel Legrand *Summer of '42*	Michel Legrand *Summer of '42*
1972	Charles Chaplin et al. *Limelight*	Nino Rota *The Godfather*
1973	Marvin Hamlisch *The Way We Were*	Alan Price *O Lucky Man!*
1974	Nino Rota and Carmine Coppola *The Godfather Part II*	Richard Rodney Bennett *Murder on the Orient Express*
1975	John Williams *Jaws*	John Williams *Jaws/The Towering Inferno*
1976	Jerry Goldsmith *The Omen*	Bernard Hermann *Taxi Driver*
1977	Jonathan Tunick *A Little Night Music*	John Addison *A Bridge Too Far*
1978	Giorgio Moroder *Midnight Express*	John Williams *Star Wars*
1979	Georges Delerue *A Little Romance*	Ennio Morricone *Days of Heaven*

Year	OSCAR®	BAFTA
1980	Michael Gore *Fame*	John Williams *The Empire Strikes Back*
1981	Vangelis *Chariots of Fire*	Carl Davis *The French Lieutenant's Woman*
1982	John Williams *ET*	John Williams *ET*
1983	Bill Conti *The Right Stuff*	Ryuichi Sakamoto *Merry Christmas, Mr Lawrence*
1984	Maurice Jarre *A Passage to India*	Ennio Morricone *Once Upon a Time in America*
1985	John Barry *Out of Africa*	Maurice Jarre *Witness*
1986	Herbie Hancock *Round Midnight*	Ennio Morricone *The Mission*
1987	Ryuichi Sakamoto, David Byrne et al. *The Last Emperor*	Ennio Morricone *The Untouchables*
1988	Dave Grusin *The Milagro Beanfield War*	John Williams *Empire of the Sun*
1989	Alan Menken *The Little Mermaid*	Maurice Jarre *Dead Poets Society*
1990	John Barry *Dances With Wolves*	Ennio and Andrea Morricone *Nuovo Cinema Paradiso*
1991	Alan Menken *Beauty and the Beast*	Jean-Claude Petit *Cyrano de Bergerac*
1992	Alan Menken *Aladdin*	David Hirschfelder *Strictly Ballroom*
1993	John Williams *Schindler's List*	John Williams *Schindler's List*
1994	Hans Zimmer *The Lion King*	Don Was *Backbeat*
1995	Luis Enriques Bacalov *Il Postino*	Luis Enriques Bacalov *Il Postino*
1996	Gabriel Yared *The English Patient*	Gabriel Yared *The English Patient*

Year	OSCAR®	BAFTA
1997	James Horner *Titanic*	Nellee Hooper, Craig Armstrong et al. *William Shakespeare's Romeo + Juliet*
1998	Nicola Piovani *Life is Beautiful*	David Hirschfelder *Elizabeth*
1999	John Corigliano *The Red Violin*	Thomas Newman *American Beauty*
2000	Tan Dun *Crouching Tiger, Hidden Dragon*	Tan Dun *Crouching Tiger, Hidden Dragon*
2001	Howard Shore *The Lord of the Rings: The Fellowship of the Ring*	Craig Armstrong and Marius De Vries *Moulin Rouge*
2002	Elliot Goldenthal *Frida*	Philip Glass *The Hours*
2003	Howard Shore *The Lord of the Rings: The Return of the King*	Gabriel Yared and T-Bone Burnett *Cold Mountain*
2004	Jan A.P. Kaczmarek *Finding Neverland*	Gustavo Santaolalla *The Motorcycle Diaries*
2005	Gustavo Santaolalla *Brokeback Mountain*	John Williams *Memoirs of a Geisha*
2006	Gustavo Santaolalla *Babel*	Gustavo Santaolalla *Babel*
2007	Dario Marianelli *Atonement*	Christopher Gunning *La vie en rose*
2008	A.R. Rahman *Slumdog Millionaire*	A.R. Rahman *Slumdog Millionaire*

Film Music in the Classic FM Hall of Fame

Every year since 1996, we have asked our listeners to vote for their three favourite pieces of music. We assemble all the votes together to create the *Classic FM Hall of Fame Top 300*. This chart, unveiled over the Easter weekend, is a living, breathing snapshot of our listeners' tastes and has now become the biggest annual survey of classical music anywhere in the world.

The list published here is of all of the pieces of music specifically written for films that feature in the current *Hall of Fame*, the number being the position in the chart of the piece of music that follows.

 32 Howard Shore: *Lord of the Rings*
 58 Nigel Hess: *Ladies in Lavender*
 62 Ennio Morricone: *The Mission*
 77 John Williams: *Schindler's List*
106 Dmitry Shostakovich: *The Gadfly*, "*Romance*"
116 Hans Zimmer: *Pirates of the Caribbean 2*
118 Dmitry Shostakovich: *The Unforgettable Year 1919*
119 Hans Zimmer: *Gladiator*
137 Klaus Badelt: *Pirates of the Caribbean*
145 John Williams: *Saving Private Ryan*
148 John Williams: *Star Wars* theme
149 John Barry: *Dances with Wolves*
157 John Williams: *Harry Potter* theme
165 Richard Addinsell: *Warsaw Concerto*
213 John Barry: *Out of Africa*
215 John Williams: *Jurassic Park*
233 Craig Armstrong: *William Shakespeare's Romeo + Juliet*
237 William Walton: *Spitfire Prelude and Fugue*
243 John Williams: *Raiders of the Lost Ark*
275 Michael Nyman: *The Piano*
284 Patrick Doyle: *Harry Potter and the Goblet of Fire*
298 Sergei Prokofiev: *Lieutenant Kijé*

Have a Listen for Yourself

It would be completely impossible to fit all the examples of the different types of film music onto one CD. The disc that accompanies this book will give you a taster of just some of the music discussed over the preceding pages.

The CD contains 20 tracks – 10 pieces of outstanding film music by some of the masters of movie music whom we've met in this *Friendly Guide* and 10 pieces of wonderful classical music that have enjoyed a second lease of life thanks to their use in a movie.

The recordings come from Naxos label CDs, two of which are no longer available. Every Naxos disc is released at a budget price and is excellent value for money so, if you want to build up a collection of great film music, you can do so without much financial risk.

Film scores

1 Max Steiner: *Gone with the Wind* (1939)

Max Steiner wrote three hours of music for *Gone with the Wind* in just three months, while scoring three other movies at the same time. It became the composer's most popular work, mainly thanks to the deeply romantic "*Tara's Theme*".

Naxos 8.990024 (no longer available)

2 Erich Wolfgang Korngold: *The Adventures of Robin Hood* (1938)

Korngold's music is always visual – you know what's happening on screen just by listening to it. This example from the Errol Flynn classic shows off Korngold's art at its swashbuckling best.

Naxos 8.558210–11

3 Alfred Newman: *Captain from Castile* (1947)

One of the greatest scores ever to come out of Hollywood. Newman conjures up the 16th-century conquest of Mexico by Hernando Cortez, played by Cesar Romero, who ended up playing the Joker in the *Batman* TV series.

NAXOS 8.990024 (no longer available)

4 Richard Addinsell: *Dangerous Moonlight*, *"Warsaw Concerto"* (1941)

A Second World War weepie, *Dangerous Moonlight* features Anton Walbrook as a pianist who has lost his memory. Addinsell composed the hugely popular Rachmaninov-style *"Warsaw Concerto"*, played by Walbrook's character in the film.

NAXOS 8.554323

5 Maurice Jarre, *Lawrence of Arabia* (1962)

It's impossible to hear Maurice Jarre's stirring music without seeing the expansive desert, and remembering Peter O'Toole's dazzling performance as T.E. Lawrence. It's a miracle that Jarre composed the whole score in just one month.

NAXOS 8.990024 (no longer available)

6 John Barry: *Dances with Wolves* (1990)

John Barry's Oscar®-winning soundtrack is as far removed from the conventional Hollywood western score as you could imagine. No rollicking in the saddle, here. This is music that depicts the wide-open plains of South Dakota.

Naxos 8.570505

7 John Williams: *Schindler's List* (1994)

One of the great movie themes of the 1990s, if not all time. Williams created a poignant violin solo that recalls the traditions of central European Jewish music and captures the desperation of the film's events.

Naxos 8.570505

8 James Horner: *Titanic* (1997)

A massive hit for Celine Dion helped the *Titanic* soundtrack top the bestseller charts. Horner cleverly mixed Celtic folk music with driving synthesizers that suggested the spirit of progress embodied in the great ship.

Naxos 8.570505

9 Hans Zimmer: *Gladiator* (2000)

For *Gladiator*, Zimmer – assisted by Lisa Gerrard –
composed a score that sounded at once timeless – as
if it could have been from the time of General
Maximus himself – and as contemporary as the
CGI effects in the gladiator ring.

NAXOS 8.570505

10 Howard Shore: *Lord of the Rings* (2001–2003)

Films don't come much more epic than Peter
Jackson's nine-hour trilogy and Howard Shore's
majestic score magnificently provided the symphonic
backdrop to all the wizardry and wonder.

NAXOS 8.570505

The Classics at the Movies

11 Handel: *Zadok the Priest*

One of four Coronation Anthems written by
Handel in 1727 for King George II and used at
every royal coronation since. The music is used to
great effect in *The Madness of King George* (1994)
and in *Breakfast on Pluto* (2005), and popped up
again in *Johnny English* (2003).

NAXOS 8.557003

12 Mozart: Clarinet Concerto, 2nd movement

John Barry rightly won the plaudits for his *Out of Africa* (1985) soundtrack but it was director Sidney Pollack's ingenious use of Mozart playing out over the savannah from an old gramophone that still lingers in the memory.

Naxos 8.570015–16

13 Allegri: Miserere

One of the most popular pieces from the late Renaissance, the Miserere is a setting of Psalm 51. Composed in the 1630s, the piece found a new audience after it was used in *Chariots of Fire* (1981) alongside Vangelis' electronic score.

Naxos 8.550827

14 Mozart: Piano Concerto No. 21, 2nd movement

The 1967 Swedish film *Elvira Madigan* gave this 1785 piano concerto by Mozart a nickname that it has been stuck with ever since. If you've seen the film, you'll remember this is the music used to accompany a relaxing boat ride on a peaceful lake.

Naxos 8.570015–16

15 Paul Dukas: *The Sorcerer's Apprentice*

The image of Mickey Mouse conducting the stars and trying to control his broomstick is so inextricably linked with this music that it's hard to hear it without seeing Disney's timeless animated sequence from *Fantasia* (1940).

NAXOS 8.551166

16 Catalani: *La Wally*, "*Ebben? Ne andrò lontana*"

The stylish 1981 French thriller *Diva* made the aria from Catalani's little-known opera, *La Wally*, central to its story of a young courier obsessed with an opera singer.

NAXOS 8.550606

17 Gustav Mahler: Symphony No. 5, 4th movement, Adagietto

Death in Venice (1971) tells the story of the last days of a composer, loosely based on the real-life composer Gustav Mahler. Visconti's use of Mahler's heart-rending Adagietto was a masterstroke.

NAXOS 8.550528

18 Richard Wagner: *"Ride of the Valkyries"*

The image of American helicopters devastating a
Vietnamese village as Wagner blares out of their
loudspeakers is one of the unforgettable moments
from Francis Ford Coppola's disturbing war drama,
Apocalypse Now (1979).

NAXOS 8.550211

19 Jacques Offenbach: *The Tales of Hoffman, "Barcarolle"*

Life is Beautiful (1997) attempted to deal with the
Holocaust from the point of view of a father who
has to help his son survive imprisonment in a Nazi
camp. The main character, Guido, manages to play
this Offenbach favourite over the camp speakers to
try to reach his wife.

NAXOS 8.550088 (no longer available)

20 Camille Saint-Saëns, Organ Symphony, 4th movement

The triumphant climax of Saint-Saëns' symphony
helped audiences cheer along the little pig that
wants to be a sheep dog in the film, *Babe* (1995).

NAXOS 8.550138

Where to Find Out More

If this *Friendly Guide* has whetted your appetite to find out more about film music, one of the best ways is to tune in to Classic FM to hear more of your favourite movie themes, in particular to *Classic FM at the Movies* with Simon Bates, every weekend. Classic FM broadcasts 24 hours a day across the UK on 100–102 FM and also on DAB digital radio and through digital satellite and cable television. You can find full details of Classic FM's programmes and times at www.classicfm.com.

If you would like to delve deeper into the world of film music and its composers, then here is a list of helpful journals, websites and publications that can assist you on your way. Enjoy the journey!

Useful movie music websites and blogs

Cinemusic: www.cinemusic.net

Film music on the web:
www.musicweb.uk.net/film/index.html

Film Score Monthly: www.filmscoremonthly.com

Film tracks: www.filmtracks.com

Golden scores: www.goldenscores.com

Internet movie database: www.imdb.com

Moviescore media: www.moviescoremedia.com

Music from the movies:
www.musicfromthemovies.com

Soundtrack collector: www.soundtrackcollector.com

Soundtrack Express: www.soundtrack-express.com

Soundtrack net: www.soundtrack.net

Stage and Screen online:
www.stageandscreenonline.com

Tracksounds: www.tracksounds.com

Upcoming film scores:
www.upcomingfilmscores.blogspot.com

Composer official and fan sites

Alan Silvestri: www.alan-silvestri.com

Bernard Herrmann: www.uib.no/herrmann

Craig Armstrong: www.craigarmstrongonline.com

Danny Elfman: http://elfman.filmmusic.com

Debbie Wiseman: www.debbiewiseman.co.uk

Don Davis: www.dondavis.net

Elmer Bernstein: www.elmerbernstein.com

Ennio Morricone: www.enniomorricone.com

Eric Serra: www.ericserra.com

Erich Wolfgang Korngold: www.korngold-
society.org/

Franz Waxman: www.franzwaxman.com/

Hans Zimmer: www.hans-zimmer.com

Howard Shore: www.howardshore.com

James Horner: www.hornershrine.com

Jerry Goldsmith: www.jerrygoldsmithonline.com

John Barry: www.johnbarry.org.uk

John Williams: www.jwfan.com

Michael Kamen: www.michaelkamen.com

Thomas Newman:
http://users.telenet.be/obelisk/tnc/

Further reading and reference

British Film Music: John Huntley, Skelton
Robinson, 1947

Film Music: Paul Tonks, Pocket Essentials,
2001

Film Music – A Neglected Art: Roy M.Prendergast,
W.W. Norton, 1992

Gramophone Film Music: Good CD Guide: Mark
Walker (ed.), Gramophone Publications Ltd,
1998

A Heart At Fire's Centre: The Life and Music of Bernard Herrmann: Steven C. Smith, University of California Press, 1991

A History of Film Music: Mervyn Cooke, Cambridge University Press, 2008

John Barry: A Life In Music: Leonard, Walker & Bramley, Sansom & Co. 1998

Knowing the Score: David Morgan, Harper Entertainment, 2000

Music for the Movies: Tony Thomas, Silman-James Press, 1997

The Score: Michael Schelle, Silman-James Press, 1999

Twenty Four Frames Under: Russell Lack, Quartet Books Ltd, 1997

Glossary

atonal   music generally lacking a tonal centre, i.e. not very tuneful

avant-garde   unusual, experimental ideas, especially in the arts

Avery, Tex (1907–1980)   American animator who specialized in anarchic cartoon shorts

Barber of Seville   Italian comic opera by Rossini featuring the character Figaro

baritone   the middle of the male voice range, lower than tenor and higher than bass

baroque era   western music dating roughly between 1600 and 1750

Barrymore, John (1882–1942)   American stage and screen actor

bass   lowest male voice

Baum, L. Frank (1856–1919) American author of books about the land of Oz

Beethoven, Ludwig van (1770–1827) German composer, a giant of western music

Berlin, Irving (1888–1989) American songwriter, perhaps most famous for *White Christmas*

Berlioz, Hector (1803–1869) innovative French composer and music critic

Bertolucci, Bernardo (1940–) Italian writer and director of *The Last Emperor*

biopic a movie telling the life story of a famous person

Blue Danube popular waltz composed in 1867 by Johann Strauss II

Bogarde, Dirk (1921–1999) British actor of Dutch descent

boogie-woogie style of American blues piano music with strong "walking bass" part

bossa nova popular Brazilian style of dance music

Boulanger, Nadia (1887–1979) influential French composition teacher of Aaron Copland

Boulez, Pierre (1925–) French composer, conductor and music theorist

Bowie, David (1947–) British singer from the "glam rock" era and actor

Brahms, Johannes (1833–1897) German pianist and composer of the romantic era

Branagh, Kenneth (1960–) British leading actor and popularizer of Shakespeare

Brel, Jacques (1929–1978) Belgian singer–songwriter with cult following

Burton, Tim (1958–) former Disney animator turned director of off-beat fantasies

Cameron, James (1954–) Canadian-born director of action movies, notably *Titanic*

Campion, Jane (1955–) New Zealander, director of *The Piano* and other art-house movies

can-can high-kicking line dance popularized by Jacques Offenbach

Cannes international film festival held at the French Mediterranean resort

Castelnuovo-Tedesco, Mario (1895–1968) Italian pianist, composer and teacher

CBS American radio and television network and record label

Chaplin, Charles (1889–1977) British physical comedian, the movies' first superstar

Charles, Ray (1930–2004) American soul singer, pianist and composer

Chevalier, Maurice French entertainer and film star, best known for *Gigi* (1958)

classical era era of music from around 1770 to 1810 including Haydn and Mozart

Clift, Montgomery (1920–1966) American leading romantic actor of the 1950s

Cocteau, Jean (1889–1963) imaginative French poet and writer

Corman, Roger (1926–) American director of 1950s horror films and B movies

Cronenberg, David (1943–) Canadian writer and director of shock horror films

Crown Film Unit   British government film unit producing public information films

cue music   music written or compiled for specific parts of a silent film

Czinner, Paul (1890–1972)   Hungarian-born director, mainly of opera and ballet films

"Dance of the Hours"   ballet sequence from *La Gioconda* (1876) by Ponchielli

Davis, Carl (1936–)   American-born composer of restored silent film scores

Dean, James (1931–1955)   American actor killed in road crash, having made only three major films

Debussy, Claude (1862–1918)   influential French "impressionist" composer

dissonance   unharmonious sound caused by clashing notes

Donizetti, Gaetano (1797–1848)   Italian opera composer of *Lucia di Lammermoor*

Dreamworks SKG   entertainment company formed by Steven Spielberg and friends

drum and bass   electronic dance music form from the late 1980s

Dukas, Paul (1865–1935) French composer of *The Sorcerer's Apprentice*

Durbin, Deanna (1921–)   Canadian singer and actress, star of musicals in the 1930s and 1940s

Dutilleux, Henri (1916–)   French composer of symphonies and chamber music

Dvořák, Antonín (1841–1904)   Czech composer of the "New World" symphony

Ealing Studios   film company specializing in quintessentially British comedies

Eddy, Nelson (1901–1967)   American singer and film star with operatic training

Eisenstein, Sergei (1898–1948) Russian director of epic dramas

exit music   music played over credits at the end of a film, as audience leaves the cinema

Faith, Adam (1940–2003)   British pop singer and actor of the 1960s

fanfare   attention-grabbing ceremonial music, played on brass

Fellini, Federico (1920–1993)   legendary Italian director

film noir   literally, black film

Fincher, David (1965–)   American director of influential cult movies such as *Fight Club*

Fitzgerald, Ella (1917–1996)   American jazz singer and interpreter of popular song

Fleischer, Max (1883–1972) and **Dave** (1894–1979)   Austrian-born pioneering animators

Flynn, Errol (1909–1959)   Australian leading star of swashbuckling adventures

Fonteyn, Margot (1919–1991)   outstanding English prima ballerina

Franju, Georges (1912–1987)   French director, set designer and documentary maker

funk   popular American dance music genre

Gance, Abel (1889–1981)   pioneering French director, founder of wide-screen techniques

Gershwin, George (1898–1937)   American composer who fused jazz and classical styles

Gilliam, Terry (1940–) *Monty Python* animator turned fantasy director

Godard, Jean-Luc (1930–)   French director and writer of the "new wave"

Greenaway, Peter (1942–)   experimental British director and writer

Griffith, D.W. (1875–1948)   the film industry's first major director

Haley, Bill (1925–1981)   pioneering rock'n'roller who had hit with *Rock Around the Clock*

Hammer Studios   British studio famed for low-budget horror movies

Hammerstein, Oscar (1846–1919)   German-born opera impresario and producer

harmonium   a reed organ with compression bellows

Haydn, Franz Josef (1732–1809)   Austrian composer of symphonies and chamber music

Hemingway, Ernest (1899–1961)   American writer of *For Whom the Bell Tolls*

Hindemith, Paul (1895–1963)   influential German modernist composer

Hitchcock, Alfred (1899–1980)   British master of suspense movies

Holst, Gustav (1874–1934)   British composer of *The Planets*, influenced by the east

Howard, Ron (1954–)   *Happy Days* TV star turned A-list movie director

Jackson, Peter (1961–)   New Zealand director of *The Lord of the Rings*

Jolson, Al (1886–1950)   American–Jewish entertainer, star of the first talkie

Joyce, James (1882–1941)   Irish dramatist and writer, author of *Ulysses*

Juilliard   school of music established in New York City in 1905

Kazan, Elia (1909–2003)   distinguished American director of stage and screen

Kern, Jerome (1885–1945)   American composer, father of modern musical theatre

Korda, Alexander (1893–1956)   Hungarian producer who "built" the British film industry

Kubrick, Stanley (1928–1999)   innovative American director based in Britain

"Largo al factotum"   Figaro's famous aria from *The Barber of Seville*

Lean, David (1908–1991)   British director of epics, including *Lawrence of Arabia*

Léger, Fernand (1881–1955)   French painter, sculptor and filmmaker

leitmotif   a musical theme used to represent or suggest a character, idea or feeling

Leone, Sergio (1922–1999)   Italian director who revolutionized the western movie

Lindbergh, Charles (1902–1974)   American aviator, author and inventor

Liszt, Franz (1811–1886)   Hungarian pianist, composer and teacher

Lucia di Lammermoor   tragic Italian opera (1835) by Donizetti, after Walter Scott

Lumière   pioneering filmmaking brothers, Louis (1864–1948) and August (1862–1954)

madrigal sung settings of sonnets or poems

Magoo, Mr   short-sighted, bumbling cartoon character, created in 1949

Mahler, Gustav (1860–1911)   influential Austrian conductor and composer

Marseillaise   patriotic French song, later became the French National Anthem

Massenet, Jules (1842–1912)   French opera composer of *Manon* and *Werther*

Master of the King's/Queen's Music   ceremonial position appointed by British monarch

Mendelssohn, Felix (1809–1847)   German composer and pianist

Messiaen, Olivier (1908–1992)   French composer and lover of birdsong

Milhaud, Darius (1892–1974)   prolific French composer, much influenced by jazz

minimalism   musical style that is generally repetitive and melodic

Mozart, Wolfgang Amadeus (1756–1791) Austrian composer of unsurpassed genius

Newman System   a way of synchronizing the musical score with a film

Nureyev, Rudolf (1938–1993)   innovative Russian ballet dancer

Offenbach, Jacques (1819–1880)   German-born composer of French operetta

Olivier, Laurence (1907–1989)   distinguished English actor of stage and screen

Ondes Martenot electronic musical instrument invented by Maurice Martenot in 1928

operetta light opera with spoken dialogue between songs

overture orchestral work played at beginning of an opera, musical or film

Pabst, George (1885–1967) German director of *Ten Days to Die* and other gloomy films

Pacino, Al (1940–) versatile American leading man of screen and stage

Pagliacci, I short 1892 opera by Leoncavallo about travelling players

Palme d'Or award presented at Cannes Film Festival

Picasso, Pablo (1881–1973) revolutionary modernist Spanish artist

Pixar Studios successful animation studio specializing in computer-generated films

Ponchielli, Amilcar (1834–1886) Italian composer of operas

prelude instrumental introduction to something bigger or a short concert work

Rachmaninov, Sergei (1873–1943) popular Russian pianist and romantic composer

ragtime syncopated piano music, popular in the USA from the late 19th century

Reiniger, Lotte (1899–1981) pioneering German animator working with silhouettes

Resnais, Alain (1922–) controversial French director of the "new wave" movement

Rhapsody in Blue Gershwin's first major "serious" work, for piano and jazz band

"*Ride of the Valkyries*" galloping tune from Wagner's *Ring* cycle

Ring **cycle** a mammoth operatic work by Wagner, a complete performance of which runs over four nights

Rodgers, Richard (1902–1979) master composer of Broadway musicals

romantic era 19th-century musical era in which emotion and expression overtook form

Rossini, Gioachino (1792–1868) hugely successful and popular Italian opera composer

Roussos, Demis (1946–) Greek pop singer with band Aphrodite's Child and solo artist

Saint-Saëns, Camille (1835–1921) popular French composer of *Carnival of the Animals*

samba colourful Brazilian dance for couples

Schoenberg, Arnold (1874–1951) revolutionary Austrian composer

sci-fi genre of fiction covering science, outer space, fantasy and alternative futures

Scorsese, Martin (1942–) consummate American director of gritty urban movies

Selznick, David O. (1902–1965) top Hollywood producer of *Gone with the Wind*

serialism composition method involving a series of notes manipulated in various ways

Sibelius, Jean (1865–1957) Finnish composer of great symphonies and tone poems

Simpsons, The American animated TV series about dysfunctional family

Sinatra, Frank (1915–1998) American popular singer and leading actor

Les Six French group of composers incorporating jazz and popular music into their works

spaghetti western distinctive westerns, produced by Italian and Spanish filmmakers

Spielberg, Steven (1946–) cinema's most commercially successful American director

Steinbeck, John (1902–1968) prize-winning American novelist; wrote *Of Mice and Men*

Strauss, Richard (1864–1949) German composer of operas and orchestral works

Stravinsky, Igor (1882–1971) pioneering Russian-born modernist composer

Sylvian, David (1958–) English singer, formerly of the "new romantic" band, Japan

Talking Heads innovative American art rock band of the 1980s, led by David Byrne

Tauber, Richard (1891–1948) Austrian-born English tenor, excelled in operetta

Tchaikovsky, Pyotr Ilyich (1840–1893) Russian composer, particularly of ballets

Thompson, Emma (1959–) English actress, formerly married to Kenneth Branagh

Truffaut, François (1932–1984) French new wave director and critic

tenor highest male voice range

theremin spooky electronic instrument much loved by horror film composers

tone poem orchestral work, usually inspired by a poetic or literary source

troubadour a poet–musician of 12th–13th-century France

vaudeville a light theatrical variety show made up of diverse performers

Visconti, Luchino (1906–1976) Italian screen-writer and director of *Death in Venice*

Wagner, Richard (1813–1883) influential German opera composer

Walsh, Raoul (1887–1980) director whose career spanned silent films through to the 1960s

Weill, Kurt (1900–1950) German-born composer of theatre music with Bertolt Brecht

Welles, Orson (1915–1985) larger-than-life director and actor, creator of *Citizen Kane*

Zeffirelli, Franco (1922–) Italian director of stage, operas and sensual films

zither plucked or struck stringed instrument, popular in central European folk music

Index of Composers

The more important references are in **bold** type.

Final Credits

I would like to express my grateful thanks to all of the friends and colleagues who made this book possible, especially: Ginny Catmur at Hodder Education, for her enthusiasm and guidance; Tim Weinberg, for his expert assistance; Simon Bates, Darren Henley and Paul Kelly at Classic FM, who during my decade on the show helped make *Classic FM at the Movies* happen every week; John Evans, Sarah Kirkup and Joanna Sallnow at *Classic FM Magazine*; and, finally, Aryan and Ashkan Ziaie, for keeping me up to date with the latest movies and enthusiastically sharing in new discoveries. To them, this book is dedicated.

About the Author

Robert Weinberg writes about film soundtracks every month for *Classic FM Magazine*. On Classic FM radio, he produced *Classic FM at the Movies*, presented by Simon Bates, from 1997 to 2007.

After graduating with a degree in expressive arts from Brighton Polytechnic in 1987, he began his radio career in the newsrooms of Northants 96 and BBC Radio Sussex. He joined Classic FM in 1994, where he has produced *The Opera Show* with Lesley Garrett and *If You Liked That, You'll Like This* and *Across the Threshold* with David Mellor. He produced Classic FM's six-part centenary series on William Walton with Humphrey Burton, the daily

176

Henry Kelly show and the *Classic FM Evening Concert.* He was the producer of the exclusive UK broadcast of *The Three Tenors at Wembley, Ken Russell's Movie Classics, The Muppets' Classic Christmas,* presented by Kermit the Frog; *Music – A Joy for Life* with Sir Edward Heath; coverage of the Lucerne International Music Festival in 1995; the broadcast from the Royal Albert Hall of Paul McCartney's *Standing Stone;* and the world premiere of Walt Disney Pictures' *Fantasia 2000.*

Television work includes *20 Operas to See Before You Die* with Lesley Garrett and *Vanessa Mae's Classical Top 10* for SkyArts. He is also the author of numerous books and articles about the Bahá'í faith and *An Opera Miscellany* (Cyan, 2007).

CLASSIC *f*M

The INCREDIBLE Story of

Classical Music

A Friendly Guide for Children

DARREN HENLEY

FOREWORD BY HRH THE PRINCE OF WALES

£5.99   ISBN 978 0340 98357 7